A PIKE
IN THE
BASEMENT

TALES OF A HUNGRY TRAVELLER

SIMON LOFTUS

Wood engravings by Jonathan Gibbs

NORTH POINT PRESS

San Francisco   1989

LIBRARY OF CONGRESS CATALOGING–IN–PUBLICATION DATA
Loftus, Simon.
A pike in the basement / Simon Loftus.
p.   cm.
Reprint. Originally published: London: Century, 1987.
ISBN 0–86547–395–1
1. Cookery, International. I. Title.
TX725.A1L64   1989
641—dc19   89-2935

For Irène

CONTENTS

INTRODUCTION

When I was seven I travelled by boat to Ireland, in the custody of a cousin, and discovered Dublin Bay prawns and black pudding. They eventually sent me back on a plane, by myself, with a label in my buttonhole in case I got lost. On arrival I solemnly declared the entire contents of my tiny suitcase to the customs officer. He let me keep my elephant.

The next year I wanted to go to Mongolia and then I decided to be a spy, like an honorary uncle who spent most of his time in South America. I delved into eighteenth century travel books, marvelling at strange engravings of sheep hitched to little trailers in which they carried their enormous tails. I pored over atlases but somehow never absorbed much sense of geography. I have only the haziest idea of the disposition of central Europe and am utterly unreliable on the whereabouts of the English counties. Nonetheless, I became an enthusiastic traveller.

Tastes and smells are often the most vivid reminders of these journeys. A fresh peach brings back a walled garden in Brittany, the smell of saffron recalls päella in Andalusia and the succulence of a watermelon evokes a dusty afternoon in Isfahan. Morocco, for me as much as our seven-year-old daughter, means couscous.

But fundamentally I am a stick-in-the mud. I always return to the same place, the house on a flooded estuary in Suffolk where I have lived since I was a small child.

HARVEST LUNCH

On the island of Inishbofin, off the west coast of Ireland, I once watched a woman climb onto a rock above a circular threshing floor and toss a basket of corn into the wind. As the grain settled on the beaten ground and the chaff blew away towards the hills I realized that I was witnessing an extraordinary sight, one of the last tasks in the most primitive of harvest cycles. In a small stone barn nearby I found the wooden flails that had been used to beat the sheaves of straw, the scythes which had mown the tiny stonewalled fields and the sacks in which the winnowed wheat, swept from the smooth ground below the rock, was stored until needed.

Even as a child I had experienced a more mechanized harvest, although those memories, too, seem from a distant past. The reaper with its flailing wooden arms was pulled by a temperamental tractor, but the old, blue-painted waggon, piled with a vast load of sheaves, lumbered down the lane behind a pair of plodding horses. I would be perched on top, high in the sky, king of my swaying castle. There was excitement at the arrival of the steam traction engine, the threshing machine and elevator, the smell of coal and corn, the noise and the dust, the heavy sacks of grain and the neatly stacked rick of shining straw. There were a great many men, it seemed, and a fulfilling sense of season, the harvest home.

The mechanization of farming, the arrival of teams of contractors in their air-conditioned combines with stereo headphones has destroyed the festivity of the harvest. It is a celebration that we now experience only on a much smaller scale, when we gather the orange pumpkins in our kitchen garden on our daughter's birthday or pick curious looking apples, like inverted pears, from our favourite tree in the orchard; or when we are abroad.

I used to go and stay, years ago, on a big, old-fashioned estate in the south of Spain where they grew and made most of what they needed, as they had always done. There were storerooms filled with earthenware jars. Biggest of all were the *tinajas*, huge Ali Baba shapes, eight or nine feet tall, that were crowded into a dark room where no woman was allowed to enter. They were filled with the strong, dry, green-gold wine (a variant of Montilla) which we drank with home-made potato crisps fried in olive oil.

The olives were harvested by families of gypsies, thirty or more plus innumerable children, who took over an otherwise unoccupied wing of the house for six weeks each year. They worked together in the olive groves during the day and at night they drank and sang and danced the flamenco as the other families on the estate crowded round the leaping fire to watch. When they had gone the olives were crushed by stone rollers into a thick paste which was spread on *esparto* grass mats and then pressed. The oil, thick and green and spicy, was stored in brown-glazed jars with flat wooden lids from which it was ladled into jugs for the kitchen.

Smaller jars held partridges and quail, packed in lard, and other mysterious preserves including our favourite *membrillos*, the quince paste that Andalucian Spain learnt to make in the Middle Ages, from the Moors. There were sacks of almonds and potatoes, strings of onions and, hanging from a beam, the ungainly shapes of the hams that José Antonio cured in a nearby salt lake. They could still remember making their own soap, from cactus, and weaving a rough cloth from the cactus fibre.

Nearby lived the brother, in an even older house with extensive stabling. He bred wonderful riding horses from Arab mares and Irish stallions. One night, after dinner, we sat drinking coffee under the arches of his courtyard. Flaming torches were stuck into brackets on the Roman pillars and his horses were paraded for our admiration. Another night it was rumoured that there was a wolf in the neighbourhood and we went out hunting for it, by moonlight.

Abruptly, twenty-five years ago, the life of these estates was altered. The price of olive oil had not risen sufficiently to cover the ever-increasing costs of harvesting, pressing and distributing it. So the olive trees were cut down and apricots were planted in their place. The gypsies came no more to sing at the olive harvest, just as cockney families of east London no longer migrate to Kent for the hop-picking, or the miners of northern France travel south for the vintage.

But there are corners of Europe where the old patterns still survive, at least in part. In a rare moment of legislative sanity, the olive tree was declared a protected species in Tuscany and its oil now commands a better price than wine, so you may still enjoy the sight of cloths being spread under the trees and families armed with long sticks beating the branches to shake down the precious crop. In Burgundy, as elsewhere in the more traditional and hillier vineyards of France, the arrival of the mechanical harvester has not yet displaced all the pickers, so I can squeeze onto a bench for a noisy vintage lunch with a lively team from the village. Gathering truffles requires the assistance of a sharp-nosed pig or hound, and you may still pass the occasional oxcart laden with the harvest, on the country roads of Italy.

Such experiences encourage a sense of seasonality which is good for the heart and essential for the stomach. To eat well, it is not enough to know that the eggs come from chickens running around the yard or that the goat's cheese has been made locally but also that *now* is the moment to look for mushrooms in the meadows and woods or to linger around friends with asparagus beds. The first Alose (shad) of the season is caught in the Gironde estuary and should be grilled over the embers of vine cuttings, disregarding the classical contempt of Ausonius, who considered it a fish for paupers. The first walnuts arrive at about the same time that the aroma of the white truffle starts drifting around the tables of every serious restaurant in Piedmont. The English, of course, have marked out their culinary calendar with puddings: from summer pud to Christmas pud by way of black-berry and apple pie. And then there are the delicacies that only make their appearance on the feast days of certain saints and others which have arisen from some quirk of the local economy. In Spain, for example, because the beaten whites of eggs were used by the thousand to clarify wine, they gave the superfluous yolks to the nuns, as a charity. Hence the innumerable Spanish recipes for egg yolks, from deliciously indecent little cakes to the ubiquitous 'flan' (crème caramel), which tastes better in Andalucia than anywhere else in the world.

For all of these things you need to be in the right place, at the right time, not somewhere else with a freezer. As often as not the right place is still to be found in France, despite the plethora of truly dreadful spots which are praised in the guidebooks. Better to rely on chance than to plan your route with a map in one hand and a copy of the Michelin in the other, because even if all goes well you will have excluded thereby the possibility of discovery, the excitement of the unexpected. My favourite restaurants tend to be those which I found simply because I happened to be there and I was hungry: the truck drivers' café that provided delicious bean soup; the station restaurant where the nineteenth century décor is matched by classical cooking of the most grandly old-fashioned sort; the posting inn into which we stumbled from a downpour to find peace, perfect service and the most wonderful food. At every level, French provincial cooking is still full of happy surprises.

One sunny, late-summer day, I was happily lost in the deserted countryside somewhere between the twisting valleys of the Maronne and the Cère, tributaries of the Dordogne. I had spent the morning tramping around a tiny peninsula at the bottom of one of these valleys, nearly encircled by a loop of the river Maronne. In the eleventh century a castle had been built on this inaccessible spit of land, whence the seigneur had sallied forth to terrorize his neighbours and to which he retreated, impregnable, to defy the king. By the fourteenth century the laws of inheritance had divided this small promontory, the ancestral stronghold, between seven lords. Each of them built himself a tower.

Like a miniature Manhattan, these towers rose alongside each other, a bare inch or two apart, as the heirs to these increasingly tiny subdivisions of land jealously marked out their boundaries and strove, building higher and higher, to outdo their neighbours. And so these brothers and cousins lived in claustrophobic proximity and violent rivalry, cooped up in their narrow towers with their gangs of retainers. There were endless brawls, knifings and family feuds. A couple of unwary paces from the protection of your own bastion and you trod on dangerous ground. The place was a microcosm of the most murderous instincts of medieval communities, riven by internecine strife but forced to unite against external threat.

Les Tours de Merle survived uncaptured throughout the Hundred Years War when all the neighbouring castles fell to the English. It was not until the time of Richelieu that these turbulent barons were finally subdued, battered into submission by an artillery train ranged on the commanding heights of the surrounding hills.

Even on a summer's day, this is a shady and melancholy place, so it was with a sense of relief that I climbed out of the valley and drove along twisting lanes through the sunny meadows of the uplands, crossed a bridge over a little stream and saw, on my left, a simple, foursquare building with a modest sign: Hôtel-Restaurant. There was no sign of life and it didn't look particularly promising, but I was ravenously hungry and stopped, determined to eat. Madame was hesitant (it was nearly two o'clock) but with a certain reluctance she showed me indoors, to a dark and musty dining room. I preferred to be outside, in the sun, so a table was laid for me on the terrace and a diffident country girl brought a bottle of wine, a jug of water and some bread. After a brief delay and without any discussion of the menu, there followed a five course meal of the simplest perfection: local charcuterie, an omelette and green beans, a salad, cheese, plum tart.

Such food is indescribable. The difference between an

ordinary omelette and that one, delicious, is to do with the size of the fork that beats the egg, the heat and thickness of the pan, the serenity of the cook. The ingredients were well combined: fresh eggs, good butter and the pleasure of the harvest, with the sweet smell of new hay drifting across from the other side of that tiny valley.

For there, directly across the stream from my table, was a scene from Breughel. Sprawled among the haycocks were three or four harvesters, dozing after their lunch and their wine. Pitchforks and wooden rakes were abandoned, bottles strewn empty, belts were loosened and legs and arms spread wide as they lay in the tiny meadow, heads in the shade of a fruit tree, feet in the sun. It seemed like a dream from an earlier age.

Then one of them stirred, yawned and stood up, an angular, gangling man whose grunt was the signal for the others. Moving heavily, still dazed from their midday break, they gathered themselves together and resumed their work, raking up the wind-rows of dried hay and piling all the smells of summer into tidy, round stacks – the height of a man.

The farmer stood for a moment looking across in my direction, pushed his cap back on his head, settled it firmly over his dark brow and with a syllable to his friends left the hayfield, crossed the bridge and mounted the hill towards me. As I finished my meal he came over, touched his cap and then tore it off and twisted it in his large and bony hands as he sat at my table. I greeted him, surprised and uncertain at this abrupt arrival, and then realized, strange as it seemed, that this awkward, narrow lurcher of a man was my host, owner of this little hotel, husband of Madame who had cooked my omelette, father of the girl who served me.

He declined a glass of wine but seemed glad to accept a 'Fine'. I struggled to make conversation: compliments on the meal; comments on the pleasure of eating out of doors on such a day; questions about the harvest. He replied with nods and short guttural noises, his twisted sickle face writhing with eager but inarticulate spasms. There were long pauses.

Suddenly he began to speak, with the explosive urgency of a man who has been silent for years. The words burst out, tumbled over each other, crowded and noisy, clamouring to be heard.

Between the dialect and the torrential force of his utterance it was hard to understand more than snatches. It seemed that he wanted to say everything at once, to express all the ideas and emotions that had piled up in his head for so long – great crashing discords, unresolved, unresolvable. Global fears seemed jumbled with entirely local preoccupations. Politics and morality, the weather and history, superstitions and hope were tangled together in so confused a way that it was impossible to determine whether he was talking about the harvest or the last judgement, the moon or sixpence.

Through it all there was a sense of strongly rooted intuition, of wildness curbed by the repetitive demands of rural life, originality imprisoned by isolation.

Then it ended, as abruptly as it began, and a smile lit up his stormy face. He drained his glass, stood up and pulled on his cap. 'Eh bien, M'sieur.' A shrug, a hand-shake and he turned back down the hill.

As I paid up and left he was working again, making hay, unhurriedly, in silence.

Pastoral idyll. But he remains as gaunt in the memory as that figure standing on a rock in the sharp Atlantic breeze, a woman winnowing corn on Inishbofin.

Omelettes

Everyone knows how to cook omelettes, but few people make them really well.

Of course you must have good ingredients – the best free-range eggs, unsalted butter – and a decent, thick-bottomed pan. But there are two other secrets, the whisk and the wave. The whisk. Beat the eggs hard with a fork *immediately* before tipping the mixture into the pan. Don't let the beaten eggs stand.

The wave. Don't fiddle with the mixture while it's cooking, making small ripples. Let the eggs alone for half a minute, then drag with the side of the fork in big waves towards the centre of the pan. Swirl pan to tip liquid into any gaps around the edges and then don't touch it again until cooked (i.e. still runny in the middle). Fold onto plate and eat.

Fillings. A pinch of salt and a grind of pepper are sufficient but I normally whisk cheese into the eggs (*freshly* grated parmesan for preference) and toss some finely chopped parsley into the pan when the omelette is nearly cooked. Or any other addition that seems appropriate. The best filled omelette that I have ever eaten was a huge one, shared by three people, which was bursting with wild asparagus from the hills of the Minervois, in southern France.

Suggested Wine Eggs are generally thought to make bad companions to wine, but cheese in the mix works wonders. I prefer something vigorous but simple – a good Minervois, perhaps, or Côtes du Ventoux.

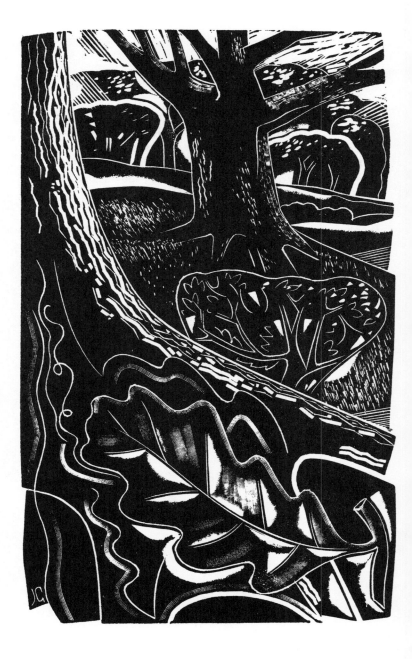

TARTUFO

In Piedmont, in autumn, scruffy men with mongrel dogs rise before dawn. They wrap themselves well against the penetrating, dank *nebbia* (the morning mist that fills the valleys of the Langhe hills) and they slip out of the kitchen door, noses twitching. This is the time of day when the scents of the countryside are freshest, when the smells of the undergrowth seep into the still air and rise gently upwards. The nostrils, too, are sensitive to the wonderfully complex aromas of the dawn, before the stronger smells of food or tobacco or exhaust fumes dull the awareness, before the warmth of the sun fuses fragrances or the wind blows scents out of the hollows of the land. Following faint paths through the vineyards, fields and spinneys, the hunters find their way to secret spots.

Under an oak tree, in the first grey light of day, the man and his dog may catch a whiff of buried treasure. The dog will probably smell it first and will begin to burrow his nose into the fallen leaves, scratching at the ground, tail twitching with excitement. His owner stoops, digs with fingers and a sharp trowel or hatchet into the soil and gradually unearths something that looks like a small, misshapen, brownish potato. But no potato ever smelt like this. As the hunter stows it carefully away, wrapped in a piece of cloth, the most intoxicating aroma fills the air, almost sickly in its rich, musky, penetrating intensity; compounded of fungal and narcotic essences, a suggestion of hashish or opium, a sniff of cheese; fresh but earthy, indescribably sexy.

This is the white truffle, *tartufo bianco*, the most expensive fungus in the world. These wonderful tubers grow in a few places in Tuscany, in an area of Yugoslavia that lies just north of the Italian border and in the heart of Piedmont, near Alba. This is their home, their kingdom.

They prefer south-facing, chalky slopes, near the roots of beech trees or oaks. They flourish at a modest altitude, in regions where the late autumn climate combines bright days with cold nights, and humidity without excessive rainfall. The *nebbia* of Piedmont is the perfect blanket for *tartufi*. Unlike the black truffles of Perigord, the white variety has not been cultivated with any success, but the spores tend to flourish for decades in the same spots, producing their annual harvest of knobbly treasures. Not surprisingly, the peasants of the region keep the knowledge of these locations to themselves, handed down in families like heirlooms, a source of income for years to come.

This secrecy extends to the business of buying and selling truffles. There is a furtive, illicit air to the shabbily dressed men who stand in small groups on the edge of the market in Alba, like pimps in the Rue St Denis. They produce their little bags of *tartufi* from a coat pocket and when they name the price it may well vary with your apparent expertise in discerning the best. Unlike the shops and the village dealers who show you a wide selection and who weigh them carefully before your eyes, computing the exorbitant price to the last fraction of a gramme, the men in the market expect you to know what you are about.

Tartufo

Sniff carefully and squeeze gently. The aroma should be pungent but fresh and the truffle ought to have a slight springiness between the fingers without in any way seeming elastic. Fewer knobbles and crevices mean better conservation of flavour. On the whole size is an advantage but don't go for anything bigger than an egg. The skin should have an apparent bloom, as if lightly dusted with cocoa, and beware of any sign of damp: a truffle that is sweating slightly is too old. Be prepared to pay a fortune.

White truffles should be eaten the day they are bought. If kept, they must be properly packed. Jane Grigson recounts the horrifying story of someone who wrapped their truffles in a bag of clean underwear, while Elizabeth David recommends sawdust or woodshavings. Both methods ignore the fact that although the truffle needs to be kept dry, it is senseless to waste the aromas by flavouring a wrapping that you can't eat. So follow the traditional Piedmontese method and pack your truffles in rice. Use a good sized jar and fill it brimful, since air space will allow for condensation. The rice should absorb most of the moisture as the truffle travels, thus keeping it fresh, and it will also be gloriously impregnated with the scent. Packed thus, the truffle will survive in good condition for three days, perhaps four.

Even sealed in its jar, surrounded by rice, the white truffle will not be exactly unnoticeable as a travelling companion. Its pungent and distinctly illegal smell will fill your car, attract the uneasy attention of your fellow passengers on the aeroplane and could cause you to be stopped on your way through Customs. They may not be amused when they unpack your treasured jar and find this highly aromatic substance which looks, at first glance, like something else.

All of which can be avoided by enjoying white truffles in Piedmont, eaten the day that they are unearthed. The ritual itself is a delight. Go into any decent restaurant in November and order a plate of home-made *taglierini*. The proprietor will lean towards you and mutter a conspiratorial enquiry 'Con tartufi?' Of course you agree with enthusiasm. A warning: don't ask the price. Apart from the fact that the answer will sour your appetite, this is as unheard of in Piedmontese restaurants as requesting a menu. Simply be prepared for the truffles to cost more than the rest of the meal.

The pasta will arrive, the finest in the world, and the *tartufi*. In a modest village restaurant they will probably bring a single specimen to the table but in a grander place you will be shown a basket of the unprepossessing objects, of various sizes, to make your own selection. The truffle is served raw, grated over your plate with a special miniature *mandolino*, until the *taglierini* are covered with the finest slithers of pale brown, lightly grained fungus, like the cross-section of a nutmeg, several shades paler. The warmth of the dish releases the aroma and the contrast of textures and tastes make this classic combination memorably irresistible.

There is much talk of eating truffles with *fonduta*, the cheesy Piedmontese speciality, but I think that's too substantial a dish. One of the best ways is with baked eggs, as I discovered in the company of Angelo Gaja (renowned winemaker of Barbaresco) at the Locanda in Neive. Angelo suggested a simple supper, ordered the eggs to begin with and chose the biggest truffle in the basket. The girl grated it over our plates, bowed courteously and murmured 'Buon Appetito'. As she turned away, Angelo called her back. 'I can still see some egg.' She brought another truffle, flaked it over the few corners that still remained uncovered and, smiling with approval, withdrew once more from the table. Washed down by Dolcetto, this was the most sumptuous simplicity I have ever enjoyed in a restaurant.

Few French gastronomes even admit the existence of the white truffle, insisting that their own black variety is without compare. This ridiculous attitude is enshrined within the pages of the Larousse *Gastronomique*, France's tedious but exhaustive version of Mrs Beeton. 'The black truffle of Perigord and that of the Lot are most highly esteemed . . . the white truffle of Piedmont has a slight flavour of garlic which goes well with some dishes.'

The man's mad. We're talking about the most pungent and extraordinary aroma in the culinary repertoire and this chauvinist pedant can do no better than 'a slight flavour of garlic'.

The Piedmontese understand the proper scale of values. I happened to be having lunch at the Locanda on the day after my supper with Angelo Gaja. The proprietor, Tonino, placed a bowl of murky liquid in front of me. 'What's this?', I asked. 'Soup,' said he, 'Black truffle soup.' Seeing my expression of disappointment, he smiled and reached for the basket of *tartufi*. Within seconds the surface of the soup was covered with a dense layer, flakes of white truffle. It was madness, and gastronomic ecstacy.

Suggested Wine Dolcetto (the 'little sweet') is a favourite grape of Piedmont, producing wines which vary from light simplicity to concentrated splendour. The best have an intense purple colour, rich fruit and a bitterness at the finish which reminds me of dark chocolate. This is by far the best wine for truffles.

ZESTÓ: MASTERING THE ART OF EATING HOT FOOD IN GREECE

> The Greeks in fact prefer their food tepid,
> and it is useless to argue with them.
>
> Elizabeth David, *Mediterranean Food*

I lived in Athens for at least a month before even noticing the truth of Elizabeth David's remark, let alone finding a solution.

Life began in the milk bar on Adrianou with a breakfast of fresh bread, Hymettus honey and a bowl of that wonderful Greek yoghurt. All of which formed a base for the retsina.

It may seem a little odd to drink retsina for breakfast but having heard that it was peculiar stuff, an acquired taste, I was determined to acclimatize myself as soon as possible. So I ordered half a bottle on my first morning in the city, found the resinous tang surprisingly agreeable and enjoyed drinking it from a tumbler. I ordered a second half bottle.

This attracted the notice of a couple of Americans seated nearby. 'Do you always drink that stuff for breakfast?' asked the girl. 'Of course,' said I, and moved to their table where we finished the rest of the wine.

One thing led to another and my stay in Athens,

planned for a few days, was prolonged indefinitely. I lived in the Plaka (still a village, huddled beneath the Acropolis), moving from a sunny rooftop to a flat in a former brothel at a suggestive address on Erotokritou, to a single unfurnished room that I rented from three elderly sisters dressed in black. Their house was crumbling gently into ruin around a weedy courtyard in the middle of which a cold water tap, the sole supply, dripped into a marble sink where I shaved each morning before accepting from the oldest sister a small cup of coffee and a pear.

This ritual replaced retsina in the milk bar. They decided, the ladies in black, wordlessly and without any gesture from me, to reorganize my life. On my first morning there I had locked the door behind me and left, as usual, for breakfast on Adrianou, taking the enormous key, which I lugged around Athens for the rest of the day before returning in the evening. My room opened onto the geranium-decked balcony which surrounded the courtyard, and as I climbed the stairs I was greeted by the oldest crone with a receipt for my rent (Greek script except for my name, copied line for line as I had written it for them) and by the sight of her almost equally ancient sisters clambering through the window of my room, carrying a bed. I rushed to unlock the door and relieve them of their burden and discovered that they had already furnished the room with a chair, a small rug, curtains for the window and a picture of the Blessed Virgin. My possessions were neatly arranged and the floor was swept. They had adopted me.

Thereafter, on my way out in the morning, I would leave the key with one of the sisters and receive from her in return a toothless smile, a cup of sweet, thick coffee and a perfect pear, green-skinned but succulent, cool and refreshing.

So I abandoned my morning bottle in the milk bar and drank my retsina instead in the afternoons, on various rooftops; poured from a tin teapot that was replenished at the nearest taverna. Occasionally, with my friends on Erotokritou, I prepared a proper meal which we took down to the local baker to be cooked in his oven and which we ate, piping hot, whenever it was ready. Mostly I survived on a series of stopgaps. A glass of ouzo, turned milky white by water, was always accompanied by *tapas*, so I chose the most generous taverna, in a quiet *platia* near the Tower of the Winds, where they provided a minia-ture feast of olives, octopus and feta cheese. Once, as an experiment, I persuaded them to serve me with *tapas* alone but the economy (it cost two drachmas instead of three) seemed insignificant compared to the loss of the ouzo. *Souvlakia* meant two very different things: those slowly turning ground-meat lumps, sweating in front of a grill, and the delicious morsels of lamb, skewered on splinter-thin sticks, dusted with herbs, grilled at a stall in the market and served with a squeeze of lemon and salad in a pouch of pitta bread. There was popcorn, exploding on braziers at every street corner and *galatapoureko*, sold from a tray.

The shops were open to the pavement and everything spilled into the streets. It seemed like a bazaar. The butcher on Adrianou could have figured in a medieval woodcut or modelled for Annibale Carracci. And the life of the street had a strong element of theatre, partly because it was the time of the Colonels, when Athens seemed the nexus not only of the particular political tragedy represented by the Junta, but also of international intrigue, personified in the curious cast of spies, racketeers and shady millionaires who gathered daily at the cafés to transact their business. Tension ebbed and flowed. At one moment the university was closed down, there were tanks in the streets, there was a bomb explosion, I was arrested and questioned in the unmarked headquarters of the interrogators. At another, the drama was on a smaller scale and the mystery comic: shutters were thrown open on a sleepy afternoon and a man stood on a balcony in his pyjama trousers, holding a cut-throat razor. Half of his chest was hairless and the other half was a bristling froth of shaving soap. He yawned, surveyed the silent street and disappeared.

Summer drifted into autumn and then suddenly it was winter. The change was signalled all at once by the brazier men who stopped selling popcorn and proffered, instead, a twist of newspaper filled with roasted chestnuts. There were still boys selling cheap plastic combs on the pavements and others pushing through the crowds, banging and shoving, laden with bails of cloth or carrying little tin trays hanging from chains (like the scales of justice) with a couple of glasses of ouzo, a water-jug, a cup of thick Greek coffee. But as the evening drew in you were more aware of the lights and the smells, of the gas flares by the chestnut sellers, the rows of bulbs in the bustling meat market like those at a fairground, and the dark brown-red unbleached wax candles in the churches, burning in heavy brass holders, their light reflected in the ornate frames and silver votive offerings surrounding the dark icons. By the church doors were stalls piled with varieties of incense and impregnated carbon blocks on little wooden trays, with battered but delicate brass scales and little incense burners, and the rich, ecclesiastical smell drifted down the street to mingle with the sweet scent of jasmine from the flower stalls and the sticky aroma of freshly cooked doughnuts.

Evening was the time for weddings. You would hear singing from a church, go in and find at the far end a bearded priest, gorgeously robed with deacons attendant, and the bride and groom surrounded by a haphazard assortment of friends, relatives and passers-by. There were no pews or seats to impede the scuttling of small children, darting across the aisles between the shadowy figures of priests and widows, dressed in black. Near the door, tables were laden with baskets filled with frilly packets of sugared almonds to distribute to the guests.

They would press me to take this gift of almonds and I could hardly refuse because the colder weather and the dark evenings had awakened my long-dormant appetite. I was ravenously hungry. So I started to eat regularly at the tavernas in the Plaka and discovered, what I had hardly noticed before, that in Greece the food is cooked once a day and served lukewarm thereafter.

Tepid *stiphádo* is not to my liking, nor tepid moussaka or *calamári*. There was never a menu at the sort of restaurants that I liked. The proprietor or his wife, father or son, cousin or uncle would recite what was available, but I soon got into the habit of walking straight into the kitchen before sitting down. That at least enabled me to see what looked most appetizing and to make my choice without any possibility of linguistic confusion, but it was only rarely that I was able to spot something straight out of the oven. So I looked in the dictionary and discovered one of the most exciting words in the Greek language: *Zestó*, meaning hot.

Thereafter life was bliss. When I accompanied friends to the taverna, they would sit down to listen to the menu recital while I headed straight for the kitchen. I sniffed and investigated the day's specialities, pointed to what I wanted and, with commanding emphasis, uttered the magic word, 'Zestó!' My friends would drink lots of retsina to compensate for the tepid food. I, too, would drink lots of retsina, to celebrate the arrival of my dish of spicy lamb sausages, delivered with a flourish, smelling delicious and piping hot.

Having unlocked this secret code, I used it with abandon and enjoyed a series of feasts. Sometimes a surly proprietor would throw me out of his kitchen but in general it worked like a charm. I explored the oldest and simplest tavernas, high up in the village, where a goat would be tethered in the yard and they only served one dish or at most two. I revisited noisier places, where the entertainment had always seemed superior to the food, and discovered that 'Zestó!' was the password to contentment. I began to think that I might stay.

So I left immediately, heading north to Saloniki, to the Turkish border, towards Persia.

A day later, I was travelling through Greece on a huge refrigerated meat lorry, trying to keep up with the driver's consumption of brandy as we drank toasts to everyone from Sophia Loren to the Queen and sang seriously out of tune above the roar of the engine. To my immense relief we eventually stopped for something to eat at a tiny, white-washed taverna on the poplar-fringed road. It was one of those crisp, bright, late-autumn days and the sense of stillness after the noise of the truck was emphasized by the wide view across an empty valley, the quiet gobbling of a few turkeys and the scratching of the chickens in the dust. A serene, apple-faced woman proffered bean soup. 'Zestó!', said I, and she put it on the stove. While we waited I watched two children playing with a cat while their mother span wool on a distaff, sitting quietly on a bench in the corner. The old woman reappeared from the back with a huge loaf of bread fresh out of the oven, wrapped in a gleaming white napkin.

Bread, bean soup and retsina. It was a perfect meal that has long outlived in my mind the gastronomic triumphs of famous chefs. It was served in peace.

Moussaka

Many cookery books give recipes for Moussaka, most of them dreadful. My version goes like this:

Slice an aubergine or two. Salt, sweat and dry the slices, then sauté until golden brown in just sufficient olive oil to prevent burning. Keep warm and dry.

Finely chop a few onions, soften in oil, add finely diced leftovers of cooked lamb (*not* beef), tomato purée, salt and black pepper, a little white wine. Simmer for twenty minutes. Stir in plenty of chopped parsley.

In a shallow dish, lay a layer of aubergine, a layer of lamb sauce, a layer of aubergine and so on.

The custard on the top is the most important part, always wrongly taught. Grate a little very hard goat's cheese (or parmesan) into a small bowl of Greek sheep's yoghurt. With a fork, quickly and hard, beat in two eggs until it's frothy. Pour on top of the lamb and aubergine and cook in the top of a hot oven until brown and bubbling. Zestó!

Serve with a few boiled potatoes and green salad.

Suggested Wine I see no point in drinking anything other than Retsina with Moussaka, but those who find this resinated white wine not to their taste could try a good but light Italian red; something like a really good Bardolino, for example. Young claret also goes well, but nothing too grand, or too old.

BULLETS AND SMASHED
HOMELETTES

Laetitia, Letitia, Letty and Lettice. It seemed for a moment, on the borders of the seventeenth and eighteenth centuries, that all the girls of the Loftus family were alliteratively linked to the same name, Latin for gladness. No wonder I can't spell lettuce. Dreaming of long dead beauties I forget the probable derivation (the French *laitue*, reminder of the plant's milky juice) and I substitute i for u: lettice.

The professionals are even less reliable. Letties, letis, letuice and lettis were the variants of a single week on the menus at The Crown, before they settled for salad. Writing a recipe or scrawling their shopping lists, chefs copy the familiar ingredients of their trade as if for the first time, like illiterate schoolboys. They have an equal carelessness with language, employing a culinary code which is full of grammatical absurdities and the jumbled elements of an oral tradition, taught by unreliable masters. Chefs mince their words, chopping and blending polyglot idioms into a mishmash of unappetizing jargon. The dominant flavour of this dialect is a form of French, so debased that it bears about as much relation to the elegant clarity of Racine as legal Latin does to the classical tongue.

The evolution of this curious vocabulary began in the mid-nineteenth century with the arrival of Alexis Soyer at the Reform Club. Of course, there had been plenty of French chefs in England before that time but they mostly worked in private households and their influence was limited. Soyer, by contrast, changed everything he touched. His kitchens at the Reform were the most advanced of the day, incorporating endless ingenious novelties, and his reorganization of English catering extended from the most spectacular public banquets to army messes in the Crimea. He was the first (in England) to establish his profession as worthy of public renown.

Soyer led an invasion of Frenchmen of varying talent, culminating in Auguste Escoffier who opened the Savoy Hotel in 1890, in partnership with César Ritz. Escoffier epitomized the best and the worst of French cooking at the turn of the century, superimposing on the vigorous peasant traditions of rural France (and the painstaking craftsmanship of his *métier*) an apparent conviction that Haute Cuisine meant truffles with everything. Historians forget that he invented the canned tomato and remember Peach Melba, which he christened in honour of an Australian soprano whose real name was Helen Armstrong. His influence was pernicious. Legions of second-rate imitators copied the forms rather than the essence of the French traditions and translated all our menus into a sort of culinary Franglais: Boudins of Fowl à la Reine, for example, or Mutton Cutlets à la Réforme. Decent English restaurants, suffering a sense of gastronomic inferiority, were overtaken by this onslaught and even felt obliged to describe their traditional specialities as 'à l'Anglaise', the derogatory designation of the French for things boiled for an extraordinary time or fried, having been dipped in egg and breadcrumbs. It also meant custard.

Such linguistic absurdities led to a monstrous game of bluff. Customers unable to understand the menu were forced into dependence on the waiters for explanation and seldom recovered sufficiently to complain if the food was awful.

Fortunately, the innate conservatism of the English villages preserved what was nearly drowned in the towns by 'French' sauces; the rudiments of simple cooking. The puddings and pies survived, as did such familiar favourites as Welsh Rabbit and Toad in the Hole: recipes and names that owed nothing to the embalmed corpse of nineteenth century France. These native traditions also flourished and evolved across the ocean, in the former colonies of the eastern United States. The American fondness for meats stuffed with dried fruit, for example, is linked by direct descent to the country houses of Elizabethan England. And the Americans also drew on more diverse traditions, from central Europe to the Caribbean, to produce Hot Dogs and Hush Puppies and Jerk Pork; snacks that offer a vivid, colloquial retort to linguistic and gastronomic pretension.

From such scraps and remnants of the past, both the English and Americans are endeavouring to reconstruct a native culinary idiom, with mixed results. The effort is bedevilled, once again, by problems of language. Having relied on French for so long, cooks lack a fluent vocabulary of English terms to describe their wares. Into this verbal gap creep the marketing men, renaming simple recipes in spurious imitation of old-fashioned country usage. Baked potatoes become 'tatties in overcoats' and Rhubarb fool masquerades as 'Mistress Hatton's country flummery'. They also attempt to persuade us that simple things like hamburgers or fish and chips or bacon sandwiches have *names*, that the *real* hamburger is called McDonald's and all others are imitations.

If copywriters can compose the menus they can also, it seems, write the recipes. At a sandwich bar in Los Angeles I sampled their handiwork. Confronted with a list of dangerous combinations I ordered a Monte Cristo, largely because it was recommended by the waitress, herself a marketing man's dream. Sandwiched in a hot, sweet, puffy bun were slices of processed turkey and ham, with 'melon chips' on the side. The whole thing was sprinkled with icing sugar and oozed with what was described as hollandaise sauce. The girl suggested topping it off with strawberry jelly: 'A lot of our regulars like it that way.'

Food like this is not funny, even in retrospect. It reminds me of motorway cafés which advertise their eggs as 'farm-fresh', or British Rail's breakfast menu which coyly describes fried bread as a crouton. There is an unsmiling commercial gleam to such laminated lists, promising food so fast that it hardly pauses between freezer and plate, microwaved miracles of portion control. Marinetti, that manic futurist (inventor of divorced eggs, green rice and diabolical roses), would have been sadly disappointed at the humourless actuality of modern mass catering. He would have been even more disgusted with the guides, the critics and the foodies, worshipping at their 'temples of gastronomy'. These places of awful seriousness have nothing to do with the good humour that is essential to good food. Their elaborate texts, honouring false gods, are engraved on enormous sheets of handmade paper, collected by the faithful and framed; momentoes as lifeless as Leporello's list of his master's conquests. Confronted by the elegant perfection of these menus, I long for the appealing inconstancy of 'letis' and its daily variants, evidence of personality, however fallible.

I love culinary jokes. How delightful to discover the Italian addiction to trifle, joy of the Englishman's heart. How doubly delightful to realize that they call it *Zuppa Inglese*, the English soup. There is even an Italian version of bread and butter pudding, dense, dark and utterly delicious. Ask in any Piedmontese restaurant for *Budino*.

Translation produces edible surprises and verbal delights. Travellers who rely on a pocket dictionary and guesswork know that the near miss is often the most calamitously wrong, but they also discover quite unexpected delicacies, not at all what they thought they had ordered. And they learn to relish that most specialized form of entertainment, the trilingual menu, studded with the inventions of linguistic mischance.

Thus it was that the Ideal Restaurant in Athens became one of my favourite places. The food was mediocre but I returned frequently to read the menu, finding delights that I had missed on earlier perusals and attempting to work out the provenance of the more bizarre descriptions. There were four columns – Greek, French, German and English. On the whole, I decided, the first translation had been from Greek to French but thereafter it had been guesswork all the way. *Keftethes* (meatballs), for example, were correctly translated as *boulettes* but appeared in English, with unexpected accuracy, as 'bullets'. Equally drastic was the originality of 'smashed homelettes' for scrambled eggs.

Even the Ideal at its most imaginative lacked the exhilarating madness of the Ramsis Restaurant in the Old City of Jerusalem. The text of this precious menu is printed in Hebrew, English and Arabic. At first, all is calm. Under 'Soups' there is a prosaic list (Veg Soup, Meat, Chicken, Lentilles). Then we come to the 'Entrance', a heading that covers a miscellany of odds and ends that don't fit elsewhere on the Ramsis Dish Menue, starting with Houmous and proceeding by way of Persily Salad and Labana Sour Milk to Jam & Butter and Chips. It's the second line which tends to arrest the attention: 'Foul', understandably unpriced. 'Drinks' and 'Sweets' lull the reader into a sense of security from which he is jolted by 'Kind of Meats': Shish Leek, Grilled Chicken, Muska Cicken and Bradised Meet with Chips. 'Oriental Food' continues this uncompromising mood, offering Manshaf, Muska and lots of stuffed things (Muttoh, Marraw, Ardshoke and Carrats with Tamer Hindi). The list ends with 'Vegetables' but there is no lapse into quiet elegy. On the contrary, the translator fights his way through the linquistic thickets with the utmost vigour, spitting out a remarkable series of tantalizing mysteries: Beens Greeiy, Green Beas, Egg Plan Twith Savle.

In a thousand years this treasured menu may be rediscovered by archaeologists and hailed as the vital clue to the decipherment of forgotten scripts, comparable in importance to the parallel texts of the Rosetta Stone. Which leads me to wonder. What if the scribes who carved that banal message to Ptolemy were as inaccurate as the restaurateur who gave us Muska Cicken? Champollion's achievement in deciphering the hieroglyphs may need revision. As a logical Frenchman, it never occurred to him that the Ancient Egyptians couldn't spell lettuce.

Suggested Wine Menus should be read with the aid of a *very* dry Martini (two drops of vermouth, plenty of cold gin) or a glass of Champagne.

VODKA AND ORANGES:
A WINTER'S TALE

It was late November and bitterly cold when I crossed the Bosphorus to Asiatic Turkey. The wailing sirens of the other ferry boats provided a suitably mournful chorus as we left behind the dirty grey, rolling oily waters of the Golden Horn and the melancholy beauty of Istanbul.

Three US dollars had bought me a third class railway ticket for the thousand mile, two-day journey to Erzerum but this did not guarantee a seat. For the first day and long cold night I was huddled in a corner of the corridor, trying to protect myself from the icy blasts which whistled through the gaps between the carriages. The land grew increasingly barren and the winter sun was reflected by snow which obliterated the country, leaving an abstract pattern of white, blacks, greys and biscuit-coloured mud. In this beautiful monotony everything was a dramatic incident: a clustered hamlet; the shaggy peasant with his donkey, alone in the wilderness; a few trees or a frozen stream.

The express train stopped frequently, apparently on request. There would be two or three patient figures waiting by the track, or a passenger would climb down and (without a backward glance) trudge off into the desolate waste. There was no station, no road, no sign of a house to mark these unexpected halts.

Some of those who boarded the train in this way were pedlars, selling everything from food and drink to handkerchiefs and horoscopes. One set up base in the opposite corner of the corridor, near the door, and I watched with interest as he plied his trade. He had two buckets, one of water and one of goat's milk. His boy would set off with a basket of bottles and return a few minutes later with the empties. These were rinsed, refilled with a mixture of milk and dirty water, sealed with a crown cap. Off the urchin would go again, pushing his way past piles of baggage into the crowded compartments. In the middle of the night the rogue smiled, winked and handed me a cup of milk, ostentatiously undiluted. A young man passed us, looking wildly around him as he edged his way down the corridor like a nervous animal. At the swaying junction between the carriages it took him over a minute to summon up courage to leap across and continue on his way.

On the second day I managed to squeeze into a compartment, exchanging the frost of the corridor for the warm stink of my fellow passengers, four on each wooden bench, two asleep in the luggage racks. After some hours of fitful dozing, head banging against the wall, a neighbour's head heavy on my shoulder, it was my turn to climb aloft for two hours comfortable slumber. I was awoken by a sharp prod in the back from the stick of a fat farmer who heaved himself laboriously up to take my place. Our bundles and bags were piled all around us and stacked in the corridor. There was no room to move and not much air to breathe but it was warm.

A young peasant looked gently at his wife, heavily veiled, as she clutched their crying red-faced baby. They were squeezed into their corner by a pair of ruffians in clothes so frayed and patched that you could hardly tell what was the original cloth and what had been added. These men seemed simple, with a repressed violence, but the farmer and his wife taught me some basic Turkish and fed me from their own supplies. The plump first class passengers had the use of a wonderful old, mahogany-panelled French dining car.

Towards the end of the journey I discovered tucked under the seat a horde of letters, documents and all the identification papers except passport of a South African, Brian Victor Crumplin. For a while I thought of adopting this unexpected mask. But I didn't like the names.

We arrived at Erzerum at dusk. Outside the station was a cluster of horse-drawn hackneys manned by ferocious drivers with huge moustaches, fur hats and bulky coats. I found myself squashed into a cab with three other passengers and a pile of baggage as we set off with great shouts ,the drivers using their whips indiscriminately on horse or rival as they raced each other across the snow-packed streets. The iron-rimmed wheels struck sparks from the cobbles and the nags fought for a foothold. We passed horse-drawn sleds, laden with crates, and glimpsed the silhouettes of veiled women crossing the street like shadows, children on toboggans and dogs like wolves.

Frozen, bruised but exhilarated I was deposited at a cheap hotel that seemed, for a moment, an oasis of warmth and comfort. There was a glowing stove and a bar, with glittering mirror-backed shelves and padlocked glass doors to display and guard the precious booze. I was prepared to stomach anything alcoholic but I had forgotten Moslem temperance. The mirage of a strong drink dissolved into the reality of row upon dusty row of Coca-Cola bottles. I settled, forlornly, for a glass of tea.

The buses into Persia had stopped running because of the dreadful weather. It was said that a snowplough had managed to get through but few other drivers seemed prepared to risk it. I hung around the bus station, hoping for news of a departure and eventually met a Pakistani who knew a Persian with a car who was leaving on the morrow.

We met the next morning, having agreed to start early, and I helped fit the snow chains with a pleasing sense of renewed adventure. The men of Erzerum stood chatting in the streets, rifles slung across their shoulders, as the sun glittered off the snow. It was cold, below freezing point, but there was an air of expectant exhilaration as if before a hunting party. By mid-afternoon anticipation had dissolved into amorphous gloom. The Persian was endlessly delayed by some mysterious business, never explained, which was resolved at last by the arrival of a crate of oranges which he stowed carefully in the boot. It seemed a trivial reason to postpone our departure until dusk, with the temperature falling fast. At night we could expect twenty degrees of frost, with a biting wind that made it seem colder still. The streets were deserted as we set off and the car moved sluggishly.

We were a strange party. Our driver was edgy and impatient, anxious to make up time. He was hunched over the wheel, pale, plump and unhealthy, with the air of a confidence trickster who had lost his knack. The Pakistani looked miserable, shivering in his mackintosh as he clutched a neatly furled umbrella and a small, cheap suitcase. He was somehow in collusion with the Persian but didn't seem happy about this, or anything else. I must have appeared odd since I was monstrously padded against the cold, wearing two of everything (pyjamas, shirts, trousers, socks and pullovers) as well as a long sheepskin coat and treasured black homburg, found in the cupboard of a deserted schoolhouse in Dublin.

Nonetheless, I felt chilled to the marrow. The car engine wouldn't warm up and the heater didn't work. We crawled along, shivering, trying to see through the thickening film of ice on the inside of the windscreen. The Persian produced a bottle of vodka and I longed for a sip, but we had to use it as anti-freeze, to clear a tiny patch to peer through. After an hour we came to a village but our driver insisted on continuing towards the border. He seemed determined to make a rendezvous.

Then the blizzard started. We could see no more than a few feet, the car would hardly move in the intense cold and several times we skidded into a wall of ice and snow. Every time we stopped it seemed less likely that we should ever move again. I could no longer feel any sensation in my extremities, my teeth were chattering uncontrollably and I resigned myself to death as I repeated a series of purely mechanical actions – pouring a small drop of vodka onto a rag and wiping, wiping at the windscreen. The first bottle was long finished and we were down to the last drop of another half-bottle that the Pakistani had reluctantly produced from his case. The car was moving at walking pace and our own reactions were so sluggish that it took us a long moment to realize, with delirious relief, that we had arrived at a village.

Horasan was full of hairy men. The only restaurant served food so vile that we ate sparingly, despite ravenous hunger. In the even shabbier hotel, half a dozen heroes sat around a stove, drinking tea. They all had tangled beards, fur hats and heavy coats – an impression of shagginess and dirt. The Pakistani and I joined the circle to warm ourselves and called for glass after glass of sweet tea to obliterate the taste of our supper and to drown the memory of the vanished vodka. The Persian had refused to eat and now refused to drink. He paced around the room demanding orange juice and occasionally he set off on a hopeless sortie into the town in search of some, ignoring the crate of fruit in the boot of his car. It seemed a more incongruous obsession in such a place than my own nostalgia for the bars of Dublin.

The hairy ones departed one by one, some into the cold, others upstairs to their beds. By the light of an oil lamp the sour-faced innkeeper led us up the rickety wooden steps, grey with dirt, and down a murky passage. Walls, floor and ceiling were the same filthy shade of grime. There were alcoves off the passage, with verminous-looking beds, and the sound of snores. A man staggered up and went to relieve himself in a corner and a large rat scurried into its hole. I decided it would be better to sleep downstairs.

We hauled down some mattresses and draped them on rows of wooden chairs around the fire. At least it was warm (the iron stove had worn so thin that we could see the embers through its glowing walls) and, I hoped, safe from the rats as we dozed on our ramshackle platforms. Every few hours the Persian would get up and go outside to start the car, trying to keep the engine from freezing solid.

In the morning he lit a small fire under the motor to warm it before we started. There was an eruption of smoke and flames from the bonnet – he had forgotten to remove the insulating layers of newspaper, now dangerously ablaze. After a few frantic moments, beating out the fire, we loaded our bags and were off.

It was a fine day, quite unlike the already distant horrors of the previous night. We climbed into the mountains, tore off the exhaust on a passing rock and descended noisily towards the plain. By mid-afternoon we were clear of the snows and could take off the chains. An hour later we passed Mount Ararat, lovely but desolate place for the Ark to have come to rest after the Flood, and for Noah a perilous descent to a harsh landscape.

Then we were at the border. We drew up alongside the Porsche of a rich young Persian returning home from a hunting expedition. On the back seat was a trayload of hawks, masked with fine leather hoods and bright plumes, fretting and pecking in their savage splendour.

There was trouble over the oranges. The customs officers started asking questions and making difficulties. Perhaps the right man wasn't on duty or hadn't been paid enough. It all seemed a lot of fuss over a crate of fruit. Were the oranges stuffed with drugs, or diamonds, or explosives? Fantastic explanations proposed themselves more readily than prosaic answers.

After an hour's argument, the Persian drove us back a few yards into Turkey and handed over the oranges to the safekeeping of an elderly Turkish customs officer, evidently a friend. Relieved of our troublesome cargo we were waved rapidly through the border.

It was like waking from a dream, a winter nightmare of mysteries and mirage. There had been a surreal, disjointed, episodic quality to the journey. It seemed that the cold had frozen the connections between one experience and the next.

Persia felt like spring, vivid with life and expectation. The land no longer had the desolate monotony of the Turkish snow. We passed small rushing streams, bordered with willows, and crossed a vast plain studded with strange outcrops of red rock, glowing in the setting sun. The next day produced a landscape equally strange, folded into hills like fossilized sand dunes. In this dun-coloured scene, the mud houses merged with the land but their flat roofs were crowned with conical haystacks.

The air was crisp, invigorating and clear. Visible at a great distance, isolated figures held the attention: turbanned men or veiled women standing with bundles balanced on their heads, horsemen with rifles, an eagle pecking at a carcass, a man plodding through the dusk with three heavy-laden camels. At the entrance to the towns there were ramshackle triumphal arches in protracted celebration of the Shah's coronation, lit like a fairground with rows of electric bulbs. The evenings were filled with the wonderful mixture of smells that drifted from the shops and stalls, where spices and fruits were weighed out on the brass pans of ancient scales.

As we approached Teheran, the roadside became increasingly littered with the wrecks of abandoned lorries. The crew of one such truck had emerged unscathed from the crash and were cheerfully brewing a pot of tea, perched like benign vultures on the pile of their tumbled load. Great flocks of sheep and herds of goats blocked the way. There were oxen drawing carts with solid wooden wheels and teams of labourers, repairing the potholes.

We skirted the corpse of a long-dead camel, an island in the traffic, and wound our way into the noisy confusion of the city. Our journey was over. Of all the mysteries of those winter days, one will not sleep, but nags away at the back of the mind, provoking impotent speculation. I no longer trouble myself about the identity of Brian Victor Crumplin or wonder how a Pakistani and a Persian found a stock of vodka in frozen Erzerum. But why the oranges?

Vodka and Oranges

Frozen Oranges

For each couple allow four oranges, a few cardamoms, an egg white, an ounce of sugar and a little vodka.

Cut the tops off half the oranges, carefully scoop out the flesh and combine with the juice of the remaining oranges. Reduce to half by boiling with the crushed cardamoms and allow to cool. Scrape thin slithers of zest off the unwanted orange skins and toast quickly in a pan. Chop into small fragments. Whip egg whites until frothy. Boil sugar with a little water for one minute (two tablespoons per ounce sugar), pour into egg whites and continue beating at full speed for three minutes. Whisk in orange juice, dash of vodka, fragments of toasted orange skin and freeze (in the scooped-out shells) for three hours.

A note of caution. If you puncture the orange skin when scooping out the flesh, the filling will seep out in the freezer.

For a richer flavour, fill the skins with home-made orange ice cream, mixed with fragments of toasted orange zest and almonds.

Suggested Wine Chilled Polish vodka.

THE MIDNIGHT BAKERY

Following an unidentifiable sound (heavy, rhythmic, gritty) I slipped through a narrow passage, utterly dark, and found myself in a small domed room, lit by a single bulb. A blindfold camel, harnessed to a wooden shaft, was plodding round and round, turning a huge millstone on a granite bed.

I licked my finger and leant forward to dip it into the whitish flour, meaning to taste, but was prevented by the miller, a thin eager man who tried to explain something and then, seeing my incomprehension, led me to a corner and showed me small bins of different coloured powders. Evidently not edible.

He took me to the yard outside, where vast cauldrons steamed gently over wood fires and skeins of wool hung in loops of creamy white on nearby poles. An enormous man, bare to the waist, dipped a rack of wool into a cauldron and drew it out, dripping deep red. Seeing my amazement, he turned to the next vat and dipped again. It was saffron. And again, it was indigo. His boy then beckoned and ran up a series of rickety ladders to the sky. I found myself in a strange landscape of bulbous shallow domes, the dun-coloured roof of the bazaar stretching away in all its complex irregularities towards the gleaming and perfect domes of the mosques, bright blue and buff pink, shining against the heat-hazed ochre of the distant mountains. And all over the warm monotone of this roof were wooden poles and racks, the dyer's frames, vivid with skeins of brilliant colours, drying in the sun.

Such unexpected wonders are like jumps in time. The blindfold camel, grinding pigments in the Great Bazaar at Isfahan, is the living memory of an almost changeless past. So, too, is the Moroccan water carrier, barefoot but resplendent in gaudy tatters, with strange hat and jangling bell, who waylays you in the square at Taroudant to proffer a tepid drink from his bulging goatskin bladder. So too the moneychangers of Istanbul.

All bazaars have this fascination but Persian bazaars are particularly evocative, since they combine the complex life of an Eastern market with a setting of ancient splendour. In Kerman, the bird sellers squat amongst their cages of pigeons below entrancing tiled mosaics of parrots and blue monkeys. In Isfahan the bazaar matches the grandeur of this ancient city, the former capital of Persia: it is built around three sides of a great square and its buff-coloured brick façade, enclosing this huge space, is punctuated by the gleaming, magnificently tiled gates of two famous buildings, the great Shah mosque and the smaller but exquisitely proportioned mosque of Sheik Lutfullah.

In contrast to the peace of the mosques, the bazaar teemed with activity and was so rich with intriguing smells that I could have found my way blindfold, sniffing the air. Aromatic spices spilled from a tiny stall, heaped on dented copper plates, in battered wooden boxes or open sacks. One slot in the wall was lined with curling scarlet slippers and the next with bolts of gaudy cloth. There were smoky streets filled with the hammering of the metalworkers, and others that glittered with brass and silver, where I picked my way through trays of beads and dusty trinkets. Behind one of the main alleys of the old bazaar there was a tiny space where two young girls sat before a loom, patiently tying the endless knots of an intricate carpet. Nearby was a carver making the wood-blocks for printing cloth by hand, with patterns unchanged for centuries. On another stall I found a box of those crude but lovely beads, glazed in the same wonderful blue as the domes of the mosques, which the nomadic herdsmen string around the necks of their favourite goats.

I used to escape the crowds, the porters with their heavy burdens, the moneychangers and vendors, and sit in the peace of the tea shop, listening to the bubbling of the water pipes and the rhythms of idle conversation.

The Isfahan bazaar had long outgrown its original tall, domed passages around the square and had extended into a chaotic warren of intriguing spaces. At one point there was an archway into a sunlit empty yard, with weeds growing between the paving, and at another I was lured into the deepening gloom of storerooms and workshops. It seemed endless and I lost all sense of direction, emerging unexpectedly into a deserted cranny behind a mosque, where water dripped from a broken marble tank under the sparse shade of a scrawny tree.

Large though it seemed, Isfahan's Great Bazaar could have been swallowed by that of Teheran, reputedly the biggest covered bazaar in the East. I spent days there, exploring without repetition, losing my way and discovering entire sectors that had eluded me. I used to wander at random, following a porter to his destination, or pursuing a beautiful girl whose expressive eyes had smiled above the hand which held the lightly concealing veil.

The Midnight Bakery

Colour and smell, noise and taste and seductive glance – these immediate sensual attractions were sufficient to draw me into the bazaar, to delight and to entertain, but the continuing, unending fascination was of a town within the city, a place where life went on in forms that had altered little over the centuries. The bazaar is both market and meeting place, a forum of social activity that brings together men and women, unites town and country. The mosque may have a more profound and dramatic influence on the mood of the nation but the bazaar is where the small patterns of daily life are most evident to the outsider.

It seemed extremely resistant to change. One of the most exhilarating things about the huge bazaar of Teheran was that it had survived in all its complex confusion, despite the strenuous efforts of the Shah to turn his capital into a tedious modern city. He demolished the old alleys to make way for grandiose streets lined with the boastful architectural gestures beloved of all dictators, and he erected meaningless monuments to his own glory, but he was unable to touch the heart or, as it subsequently transpired, the soul of the city.

I was constantly delighted by the continuity of ancient habits, often in incongruous juxtaposition with the new. In the lane beside the grand central post office, for example, sitting in its shade, were the scribes. With their impressive array of pens, paper, seals and well-thumbed books of epistolary formulae they seemed like disreputable father confessors as they listened to their clients and translated the whispered confidences of illiterate correspondents into the traditional phrases of filial respect or a flowery declaration of love.

Even more incongruous was the fact that one of the oldest of Persian rituals could only be witnessed in a strange octagonal room, hidden within the opulent marble headquarters of the Melli Bank. Here, to the accompaniment of chantings from the Qur'ān and the music of drums and bells, a team of men wearing wondrous breeches (embroidered with texts and arabesques) swung huge clubs, weighted with lead; tossed a great steel bow with crashing iron chain; danced like dervishes. This was Zurkaneh, a series of ritual exercises dated back to the earliest times.

The more I explored the city, the more I discovered that behind the ugliness of the modern streets and the crazy traffic, there survived the extensive warren of the eighteenth century town, a maze of narrow lanes between blank, mud brick walls, pierced here and there by a doorway surrounded with complex decoration. There were barrel-vaulted passageways and the constant suggestion of unseen gardens; the scent of blossom, or the branches of a tree leaning over the alley wall.

During the day those alleys were always half asleep, often deserted, but at night they awoke. The city then (before the Ayatollah) had an air of gaiety and the cloak of Islamic orthodoxy was worn lightly, like a veil. The mosques were points of orientation in the maze, just as the calls from the minarets punctuated the day, but the Moslem calendar (at its moment of annual austerity) did not settle like the camel's blindfold on the life of the town. On the contrary, it merely shifted the diurnal rhythms, so that night was day.

One evening, late, I found myself near the British Embassy, but turned off into the narrow streets and stopped at an open shop, drawn by the smell of baking bread. It must have been past eleven but they were still busy, with customers coming to buy and staying to warm themselves before the glowing mouth of the open oven. It was huge, deep, with a sanded floor, and the baker used a long wooden shovel to flick in the dough and to fish out the hot bread which was round and about an inch thick, like a fat pizza. After watching for a while, I was invited by the off-duty bakers to join them on top of the brick oven where they squatted on a fading carpet, chatting and drinking tea.

Crouched in the warmth, answering the most complicated questions with smiles and shrugs, I felt ready to subscribe to the fire worship of Zoroaster.

At which point, as in a surreal dream, a customer arrived looking like Monsieur Magritte. He told me, in French, that I should step down the street to visit another bakery.

Curious, I followed. The oven was a brick sphere, plastered smooth, with a round opening near the top and a flaming gas jet inside. It was *extremely* hot. There was a team of five men, working with the rhythm of a jazz band. The first made the dough, shaping it into round balls. The second flattened these balls into thick pancakes. The third, the virtuoso, working at intoxicating speed, rocking like a drummer with his eyes half closed, seized a pancake of dough, tossed it, pulled it in the air and slapped it on the table to flatten it further; took a huge iron comb, dipped it in water, sprinkled and pricked the thin dough, which he then flipped onto a rubber pad the size of a cushion. With this in his hand he leant into the oven and hurled the dough onto the sides or roof of the sphere, where it cooked in thirty seconds. The fourth man whipped it out with a long iron hook and the fifth man sold it.

This strange bread was piled on the counter like dead leaves, two and a half feet long, curling slightly and full of holes; unleavened, dry and rather salty.

It was past midnight, but still the third man drove his fellows on, dancing to his inner frenzy, baking bread for ghosts.

Within a few minutes the entire batch had been sold, as a stream of customers came to the door. After the soul's purification, the stomach's ease; for this was that movable midnight feast, that strange extended carnival, the mad nocturnal month of Ramadan.

Bread

I'm no baker – if I gave a recipe here it would be stolen from somewhere else. The truth of the matter is that I seldom think home-made bread is as good as that from a decent professional but I keep such heretical views to myself. I'm also a secret addict of white bread, much to the disgust of family and friends. The best bread in the world is served in Harry's Bar in Venice: rolls so delicious that it requires enormous willpower not to chain-eat. Fortunately the prices there are so extortionate that regular visits are out of the question.

Only the English could have invented delicious puddings which depend on using up stale slices of white bread, but summer pud and bread & butter pudding are both irresistible.

Suggested Wine Summer pudding is ideal with a fine Moselle Spätlese, scented of fruits and flowers, from a top estate like the Bischöfliches Priesterseminar. Bread & butter pudding needs something heartier: a glass of Marsala from de Bartoli, or that extraordinary wine from the Veneto, Vin de la Fabriseria de San Rocco, made by Renzo Tedeschi. The sweetness is defined by a refreshing acidity and a slight almond bitterness at the finish.

FRIED EGGS AND CHAPATIS

Edible history is the most vivid testimony to vanished empires. The last steam locomotive from the railway works at Crewe will eventually grind to a halt in the subcontinent, irreparable even by the standards of Indian ingenuity, and there may come a day when it will no longer be possible to recognize a Scottish face behind the counter of National Grindlays Bank in Karachi. Artefacts and institutions disappear, but the gastronomic archaeologist will still be able to trace the influence of India in the English addiction to curry and to find, as I did, that the most poignant evidence of our former glory is the survival of porridge in Pakistan.

The discovery was made in a small village of mud houses on the edge of the desert, where I arrived late at night in a sandstorm. We had been travelling all day from Zahedan, in south-east Persia, a monotonous journey through a landscape of dirty shale, rattling over the corrugations and potholes of an unsurfaced road. By early afternoon we found ourselves in a vast empty space, dun-coloured and featureless, across which the road meandered to the horizon. In the middle of this desert was a large military tent and a white awning, under which a few Pakistani officials were drinking tea. This was the border and someone had begun to draw the line

on the ground, marking the boundary with white painted stones, but had abandoned the effort after a few yards. A chain across the road formed a token barrier.

Curiously enough, the flies recognized the political geography. I had hardly noticed them in Persia but as soon as we crossed to Pakistan we were assailed by a dense cloud, black and biting, and from this point onwards they never left us.

It was dark and nearly midnight when we came to the village of Dalbandin. Sand filled the air and the *dak* bungalow was locked, but eventually we found the old *chokidar* who let us in. I never ceased to be amazed by these government Rest Houses, built for visiting officials in the days of the Raj and maintained thereafter to serve the needs of occasional visitors. Havens of the thirties, we found them in the most unexpected places, furnished with decent beds, chintz-covered armchairs and solid English plumbing. The service, too, seemed a survival of another age. That night we asked, with due diffidence, whether it would be possible to have something to eat. Fifteen minutes later the old man reappeared with two boys bearing trays of supper – tea, fried eggs, potatoes and tomatoes, brown bread and butter. Memories of Yorkshire.

The night was intensely cold and my rest was disturbed by loud snorts from below my bedroom window, but it was too dark to make out what sort of beast or rascal had taken shelter there. I eventually drifted into sleep and dreamt of the Raj. Dream became reality as bearers woke us, bringing logs. They lit fires in every room and placed jugs of hot water on the washstands. Shaved, refreshed and wrapped against the chilly morning, I went to explore.

Two grumpy camels, the nocturnal snorers, were

kneeling in the sand behind the bungalow, together with a couple of boys, twelve or fourteen years old. They had evidently taken shelter there from the sandstorm and were now preparing to be off. The boys had the mischievous air of joyriders, swaggering like adults, and there was no sign of any baggage. Perhaps they were camel thieves.

Breakfast was announced at eight by the arrival of the *chokidar*, followed by three or four bearers carrying trays. The meal was an intriguing mixture of traditions: the fried eggs were served with chapatis and preceded by porridge. We seemed, indeed, to be living in an earlier time than the rest of the impoverished village, cosseted in our Rest House, lapped by sand dunes. The lawn was green, the flagpole white, the palm trees grew in straight lines and there were enormous goldfish in the pond. Five servants waited on us, including one who did nothing but sweep the steps as soon as we trod on them. The bill came to four shillings a head.

As we were leaving, the *chokidar* asked sadly, 'When are the British coming back?'

Breakfast on an equally imperial scale was served me a few days later at the railway station in Lahore. In the confusion of the arrival of the overnight train from Karachi, with passengers trying to climb through the windows and competing with red-turbanned porters for their baggage, my wallet was stolen. I lost all my money, lists of useful addresses, my driving licence and a permit to study in the Print Room of the British Museum. So I went to the Railway Police. 'Well, my dear Sir,' said the courteous officer, 'You must understand that there are many poor people here and they are tempted to theft. It will be quite impossible to apprehend the criminal but I shall take down the particulars for the record. Would you like some breakfast?' He clapped his hands and a few minutes later I was tucking in to tea, eggs, toast and marmalade. My momentary panic at being marooned and penniless, thousands of miles from home, was entirely forgotten. Fortified by the breakfast, I was able to ignore the condescension of the British High Commission ('Terribly sorry old boy, we haven't got any lolly. I believe the usual procedure is to sell something') and to relish the fact that I was finally rescued by the Salvation Army, who gave me a bed and a few rupees to tide me over.

A week later, having sold my camera, I went to the races and wagered my subsistence on a series of elegant horses ridden by incompetent jockeys. It was a lovely place, with perfectly green grass, perfectly white railings and a spreading tree under which dignitaries of the Lahore Race Club sat behind a table laden with silver trophies. After losing steadily all afternoon I spotted a promising horse in the ring before the final race and bet my shirt on it, emptying my pockets of every last rupee. It was a foolhardy move but the horse had the sense to ignore its rider, paced itself well and stormed home to a sensational finish, half a length ahead of its nearest rival. I lived for a month on the proceeds.

This balmy day at the races, just before the turn of the year, was my last in Lahore. It was suffused, even at the time, with a sense of nostalgia which has grown stronger in the memory. Glimpses of an unknown but familiar past, images of pre-war England, were mingled with the jostling, crowded reality of provincial Pakistan.

Lahore itself is a particularly bizarre blend of indigenous tradition and colonial extravagance. The old city contains a tremendous Fort, a huge Mosque and a wonderfully noisy, smelly, colourful and chaotic Bazaar. The buildings of the Raj, by contrast, provide an extravagant summary of English architectural history and imperial fantasy. The parish churches, naturally enough, are Victorian Gothic, and the administrative offices are housed in the decent order of neo-classicism, but the rest is a riot. In the middle of a splendidly English park beside The Mall I fell asleep after Christmas lunch and awoke to a cricket ball in the ribs as a ten-year-old batsman hit a six. I gazed with a confused sense of dislocation at a large building on the boundary, a stucco chunk of Carlton House Terrace, labelled MONTGOMERY in giant capitals on the cornice. The railway station attempts to recreate Windsor Castle in red brick and then there is the High Court of Justice, most fantastic of all. I think it's one of those cases where the drawings got muddled up, something that happened frequently in Victorian England (churches were built as public baths, and vice versa). The High Court obviously started life as a cricket pavilion, designed by a schoolmaster whose heart belonged to Gothic but who was prepared to make concessions to Islamic taste. Horrendously magnified in red brick and grey stone, its effect is startling, especially as I first saw it on Christmas night, picked out in red, blue, white and green by batteries of coloured floodlights, with the scales of justice outlined in flickering neon like an advertisement at Piccadilly Circus.

These architectural incongruities may not have resulted in anything as beautiful as the creations of the Mogul emperors at Agra and Fatepuhr Sikri, but they are immensely enjoyable. Lahore is a good place to arrive but the most eccentric and delightful expression of Englishness is Simla, product of a colonial nostalgia strong enough to build a Victorian country town on a steep ridge in the Himalayas. Above the half-timbered almshouses, the lending library and the Puginesque parish church with its stained glass windows, monkeys chase parakeets through the rhododendrons and a signpost points north to the snow-capped peaks: 'Tibet 30 miles'.

The Empire left behind it a rag-bag of legacies. Some survived in incongruous circumstances, like this town in the hills, and others have taken on a surreal, Dadaist character, transformed by haphazard displacements.

Indian English is imprinted with historical curiosities; it preserves the formal written phraseology of the nineteenth century administrators, sprinkled with upper class Edwardian slang, rather than the common, spoken idioms of any epoch. Notices in the railway stations, political speeches and leading articles in the English language press share this imperial tongue. It confirms my childhood suspicion that only provincial officials, with heavily accented self-importance, ever spoke in the measured cadences of Cicero; the Romans rattled along with more verve and less grammar.

As the Roman empire disintegrated, language, customs and symbols evolved in unexpected ways. The finely modelled image of a charioteer on a Roman coin, for example, was eventually transformed into an abstract pattern, quite unrecognizable but somehow more vital than the original. Much the same process was at work on the legacy of the Raj. I saw a couple of camels harnessed to an ancient English plough and two hump-backed cows pulling a lawnmower across a well-watered lawn. Unplayed bagpipes were flourished by the village bands in a Sikh procession which included elephants and spear-wielding cavalry. A 1930s Morris con-rod, the solitary spare part in a repair shop at Ambala, was optimistically produced as the answer to a serious breakdown.

They lifted the damaged engine out with a block and

tackle suspended from a convenient tree and agreed to make the replacement parts on a pre-war lathe. We stayed at the Rest House and played bridge every night in an effort to live up to the expectations of the *chokidar*, an amiable man with an enormous moustache who tolerated a late breakfast (more porridge and marmalade) but served high tea promptly at six. We basked on the roof, read ancient thrillers in the drawing-room or wandered past the potted palms on the veranda to a luxuriant garden, full of chipmunks, parakeets and cockatoos. Our peace was only once disturbed, by the arrival of a government minister (in black limousine, with machine-gun-toting bodyguard) to confer for a couple of hours with an important Sikh.

They met each other in the neutral grounds of the Rest House and discussed their differences while sitting in chintz-covered armchairs around the bridge table. These scraps of our imperial past, I increasingly felt, were what gave a sense of unity to a fractured subcontinent. It seemed like a map made of mud, cracking as it baked in the sun. Fissures appeared after Independence, splitting a vast country into three, but other cracks have continued to divide and subdivide. There was a move to replace English with Hindi as the official language of India. 'We demand equality for all fourteen national languages,' responded the graffiti.

Such arguments expressed what I found invigorating, the rich diversity of cultures, peoples and languages. Travelling across Pakistan, meandering through India, down to Ceylon and back, I was constantly struck by the scale and the dramatic variety. What has gradually surfaced in the memory is an even stronger awareness of the vast underlying unity, the land itself.

All the more impressive, against the massive inertia of

so huge a place, are the lasting effects of British Imperial rule. In many curious ways, English culture was revitalized in India, as it was by the Irish. There are entertaining parallels. 'Have another slice of toast,' said the policeman, as he interrupted for a moment our leisurely conversation about Shakespeare. It could have been Dublin; it was actually Lahore.

Fried Eggs

Use the best olive oil and grind some black pepper over the eggs before they finish cooking. The bottom of the white should be beginning to crisp; the yolk must be soft. Don't flick oil over the egg or turn it.

Fried eggs are good with bacon and with the very best, small, boiled new potatoes. And salad. The vinaigrette should be made flavoured with a few drops of walnut oil or sherry vinegar.

Such a combination makes a light lunch. For breakfast, I prefer my eggs poached.

Suggested Wine A small glass of the finest, old, *dry* oloroso sherry. Such classic sherries are not easy to find, but are still produced by traditional *bodegas*, like Valdespino and Hidalgo. Be prepared to pay rather more than the advertised brands in order to taste these glories of Jerez – dry but nutty, rich but refreshing, stimulating, gloriously old-fashioned. One glass is enough.

GENTLY STEAMING

I have been an enthusiast for slow trains since childhood, having been brought up on stories of the Southwold Railway which meandered along the beautiful estuary of the Blyth, from Halesworth to the Suffolk coast. Built on the cheap, in 1879, it was said to have taken advantage of a cancelled export order for a narrow gauge railway in China, whence they also recruited their first foreman. The little engines and the wooden carriages were delightful, but the freight business suffered from incompatibility with the mainline system: every goods waggon had to be unloaded at Halesworth and laboriously re-packed, rather than shunted from one line to another. The railway closed in 1929, much mourned by all who appreciated its eccentricities. My own memory is second hand, passed down by my father. He used to tell how the trains went so slowly that it was possible to jump down from the open veranda of the front coach and climb on board again at the rear, having picked a bunch of daffodils from the embankment. The official speed limit for the line was 16 m.p.h.

Travelling, it seems to me, should either be at such a leisurely pace, with no sense of urgency, or at a headlong charge. At the age of seven I used to mutter 'Sä Yabonah' under my breath whenever we set out on a journey and I still find myself doing so. According to a favourite childhood book about the nomadic tribesmen of Mongolia it was their most exultant cry: 'Sä Yabonah! (Let's Go!)', they would shout as they leapt onto their sturdy ponies and galloped away across the steppes.

In Ceylon, island of elephants, these contradictory but compatible enthusiasms were combined. Travel either had a gentle gait, the elephant's walk, or was dangerously melodramatic, the maddened elephant's charge: there was no middle way. Thus the ferry to the island nearly capsized as passengers were hurled from one side of the deck to the other by giant waves which battered the boat and drenched us all to the skin, while the ferry back to India glided across a becalmed sea; even the air was still. Ceylonese buses careered at breakneck speed around the hairpins, trying to catch up with the impossible schedules imposed by the latest minister of transport. There were horrific accidents. Ceylonese trains, by contrast, puffed gently to their destinations.

The slowest that I ever experienced was that between the ferry beach at Telemainar and the capital, Colombo. It left in the afternoon and could easily have covered the distance (a couple of hundred miles) before nightfall but for some inexplicable reason it never exceeded twenty miles an hour. We passed through lush jungle, dense with tropical trees and flowers, and through little clearings with huts and paddy fields. A family was harvesting with sickles and wooden pitchforks. It was clear that they were poor, undernourished and that the work was hard but they sang together and waved as we passed. In another clearing there was a threshing floor, with water buffalo trampling in circles on the rice crop, separating grain from straw. The mixture of rice and chaff was carried in a wicker basket to the top of a rickety wooden tripod and tossed into the air. We were swallowed once more by the jungle. Butterflies fluttered by and in a stagnant pool a log stirred, opened an eye and became a crocodile.

As evening fell, the sounds of the forest increased to a cacophony of squeaks and chirps and croaks. The train stopped. After a while it was apparent that we were not expected to move again. We stayed there, nowhere in particular, until daylight allowed us to steam into the capital to be greeted by the station master who had by then finished his breakfast.

Colombo's combination of squalor and elegance, its unreliable charm, reminded me of Dublin. Even at my impoverished level (a bed at the Seamen's Hostel) it was possible to eat lobster every day and to enjoy a glass of gin in the faded colonial splendour of the Galle Face Hotel. On the beach opposite the hotel an old kitemaker took advantage of the sea breeze to fill the sky with his wares, thirty foot paper tails streaming vividly through the air. There was talk of trouble with the Tamils but this was long before tension turned to violence and the days had the innocence of a children's story book, full of Capital Letters, like Babar.

I took another slow train, climbing up the spectacular route from Colombo to Kandy to visit the Temple of the Tooth. This was guarded by huge carp, swimming idly from one morsel to another, tossed them by pilgrims. A couple of miles out of town was the Elephants' Bathing Pool. After working all day carrying lumber in the humid forest, the elephants were led down to the river where they subsided with a tired splash into the sandy water, rolled over onto their sides and dozed peacefully while their mahouts scrubbed them. Then, refreshed, they sprayed each other with their expressive trunks, like children playing in the bath.

At Anuradhapura, ancient capital of Ceylon, the Sacred Bo Tree was covered with scraps of cloth, flags of supplication. The lovely undulating grassland is studded with stones and carvings and *stupas*; dome-like temples rising in pastoral eroticism amongst splendid trees. In the oldest temple there are winding stairways in the rock, carvings of elephants and lovers and a vast Reclining Buddha, taking a thousand year rest. In the shade of an enormous tree was an open-air kitchen: clay stove, smouldering logs, earthenware pots, the smell of spices and tea.

Despite the beauty of the journey, the boat to Rameswaran, in southern India, served as Charon's ferry to Hades. Night in the railway waiting room was filled with bad dreams and the company of a thousand mosquitoes. I rose before dawn and walked through the gradually waking village to the Hindu temple. Dogs scavenged in the darkness, there was the occasional glow of a pipe, sleeping figures were huddled in doorways. Half a dozen emaciated and vociferous beggars clamoured for alms on the steps of the temple, inside which the demons of the night crawled on every carvable surface: dead chickens; grotesque, monstrous, gaudily coloured gods; erotic dreams. The place was huge, a maze of courtyards and gloomy passages lit by an occasional bulb and the gradually lightening sky. A small elephant, painted with blue patterns on head and trunk, was chained to a stone. A man appeared, slung a rope of bells around the elephant's neck, loosed the chain. Together they wandered off down the passage, clanking in the gloom.

As I walked back to the station, women were emerging from the mud brick houses to draw elaborate patterns on their doorsteps in powdered chalk, prayers for the new day, banishing the ghosts of the night. The dogs had started to bark, chickens scuffled in the dirt and pony carts raced clattering by.

On the long train journey to Madras, on the hard wooden slats of a third class carriage, I ate nothing for two days but a bunch of bananas, an unintentional but appropriate penance that honoured the starving poor of the city. Madras stank from the open sewers in the fœtid delta, steaming in the heavy, humid air. I had been there a few weeks earlier, living in a poor quarter, but now there was an International Trade Fair in progress, and the beggars had poured into town. What had earlier excited pity, now provoked rage. There was wretchedness and squalor on every pavement, famine, mutilation and disease. It seemed like hell, the more so because much of this misery was quite evidently the product not of malign circumstance alone but of conscious, deliberate cruelty and neglect. But there were comic elements amongst the tragedies. A conman relieved me of ten dollars with a story so preposterous, but so beautifully timed, that I still smile at the memory.

I escaped from the underworld on the S.S. *Rajula*, bound for Singapore. The steamer was built in the twenties, with straight sides and plenty of rivets, reminiscent of Conrad. Westerners were not allowed to travel 'deck class', so I and a few fellow travellers lived in colonial luxury on the cabin deck. In the heat of the day we played Monopoly in the smoking room, watched by a silent but wide-eyed cluster of Sikh children, topknots on their heads, until eventually we adjourned for dinner. The captain got drunk, with and without us, and the long-suffering first officer supervised the loading of the cargo at our numerous ports of call. There was always a tremendous bustle of boats and barges and shouting and smells, sometimes at night, by floodlight, sometimes at dawn. I remember one gusty evening, anchored off a palm-fringed shore, when a cluster of caïques with sickle sails, pale against the dark sky, heaved alongside on the stormy seas to unload a cargo of onions.

The food, like the ship, was a relic of imperial India. The menu offered brown Windsor soup, roast beef and Yorkshire pudding, as well as Indian dishes that reminded me of childhood curries, mildly spicy and inexplicably English. There were numerous courses at every meal, four meals a day. We ate the lot, including a series of puddings that have survived elsewhere only in the memories of very old men and in the earliest editions of Mrs Beeton.

On alternate nights, after dinner, they showed films on deck, projected onto a flapping screen below a tropical moon. Complex Indian romances took turns with dated black and white English thrillers. Neither commanded much attention. We passed an island, floating below mountainous clouds which were silhouetted like the ramparts of a Gothick castle by flashes and balls and streaks of lightning, exploding silently in the darkness.

By day we leaned hypnotized over the side, staring into the blue of the Indian ocean as flying fish flitted through the spray. Time was suspended.

Such journeys evoke the long, dreamlike days of childhood, absorbed in the moment, unconscious of the future, intent, abstracted, drifting.

Devilled Spuds

This is an ideal expression of Anglo–Indian enthusiasms.

Clean and parboil new potatoes.

Prepare mixture of fresh yoghurt, ground cumin seeds, turmeric, black pepper and a little ginger.

Coat the parboiled potatoes with the yoghurt and spice mixture, stirring in a large bowl with a wooden spoon until well covered. Turn into a roasting tray with a tablespoon of olive oil and a very little of the meat juices (if available). Roast in a hot oven. Sprinkle with plenty of chopped parsley and serve with Bulcamp lamb (see next recipe) and spinach.

Suggested Wine Good red Graves (from Domaine de Gaillat to Domaine de Chevalier) is ideally suited to partner such food, having the necessary strength of character, plus elegance. I also very much enjoy Teroldego, the wonderful north Italian grape grown in the Trentino. My favourite example is made by Conti Martini.

SHOOT A SHEEP FOR
BREAKFAST

Everyone was gambling in mining shares. They talked about it from the moment that I landed in Adelaide. Bus conductors and taxi drivers swapped tips with their passengers; barmen discussed share prices while pulling pints. It was like the Gold Rush again, except that no one cared about the minerals – it was the stocks which leapt in value, doubling, quadrupling in a week. The slightest rumour of a successful survey was enough to make unknown companies the talk of Australia. This was the South Sea Bubble, an entire country caught up in a frenzy of speculation. As I travelled west, towards Perth, I passed Iron Knob, a mountain of ore that was being sliced up by enormous machines, loaded into freight trains and exported to Japan. About half of it had already gone. Further north there were rumours of new mines being opened up, of fabulous wages being paid to anyone prepared to sign on for a three month stint. In the middle of the Nullarbor plain, half way across a four hundred mile stretch of unsurfaced road, turned to a bog of red mud by torrential rain, we waited at a lonely bar for our bus to be hauled out of a skid which had sunk it axle-deep across the highway. There was a buzzing in the sky and a helicopter appeared, altered course towards us and landed. The passenger jumped out, bought a packet of cigarettes at the bar and was off again; another millionaire on his way to a meeting.

I arrived in Perth with five dollars and a determination to get a job in the mines. I was too late. Every company, it seemed, had just recruited a small army of miners, the quotas were full. Faced with the urgent necessity of finding work, that day, I went to the Employment Office and invented some agricultural experience. I wanted to be somewhere isolated, without the need or opportunity to spend my earnings. A farmer arrived; a short, shifty miserly fellow who haggled over my pay, made a few disparaging remarks about the English and took me on. He arranged to collect me when his wife had finished her shopping and to drive me to his farm, near Pithara.

Later that afternoon I was introduced to Mrs O'Dea (double his size) and to another newly hired hand, an idle Australian. We climbed into the back of his pickup and headed north. I had no idea of distance or geography so was quite unprepared for the hundred and fifty mile journey. Cold, dusty and exhausted, I hardly noticed my surroundings when we finally arrived but unrolled my sleeping bag in the shearers' shed and crawled into it.

At seven thirty the next morning I was driving a tractor for the first time in my life, being taught to plough a straight furrow. Half an hour later I was in the paddock, on my own. These fields were huge – over a thousand acres apiece – and I felt, at first, overwhelmed by the desolate vastness of the place. We were miles from the nearest house and every tree was a landmark in this great plain which stretched almost featureless to a far horizon. It was poor soil, virtually sand, exhausted by the mono-culture of wheat, fertilized by tons of superphosphate. In parts it was poisoned by salinity, and seeped into salt soaks, reflecting the enormous sky in lifeless water. The few trees were varieties of eucalyptus, which never grew very tall in this arid and infertile place. As I ploughed in concentric circles, patches of two hundred acres at a time, I treasured every rock or gradation in colour of the soil, from grey to red to dirty yellow, every change in contour, however slight, every trace of locality. It took weeks for me to identify as a hill the almost imperceptible slope, despite eyes which were accustomed to the low lying land of East Anglia.

Gradually, however, I began to relish the space, the scale, the shadows of the clouds passing across this enormous landscape, the glow of the gum trees in the evening light. Alone on my tractor I ploughed round and round in ever diminishing rings until I reached the centre of my patch and then diagonally out to each corner and back, erasing the uncultivated crescents which the discs of the plough left at the turns. I became proud of my expertise, working a twelve hour day with only occasional breaks to refuel the tractor, replace a worn disc on the plough or munch a sandwich. I came to know where I might find an iguana, lurking like a miniature dragon in the shade of a rock, and I became accustomed to the harsh cawing of the flocks of red and grey galahs. In the evenings I looked out for the white cockatoos, flying around the house.

O'Dea bought another farm, thirty miles to the south, and sent me down with his son to clear a large tract of virgin scrub. It was hot, dusty, dangerous and exhilarating work as we drove across the land on two powerful crawlers (caterpillar tractors) with a ship's anchor chain stretched between us, uprooting everything from bushes to small trees. We charged straight at the larger trees in our mighty machines and emerged in a shower of leaves and falling branches, miraculously unscathed despite the absence of protective cab or canopy. Ahead of us as we worked were dozens of kangaroos, jumping through the bush as if herded by sheepdogs to new pastures. Curiously, they seemed not to resent us but would come closer to our noisy crawlers than to a man on foot. Once I knocked over a tree and found the air filled with an angry buzzing swarm, as a nest of wild bees fell with the branches. It was my only moment of panic. I jumped off the crawler and ran for my life.

In four days we cleared a thousand acres, burning the debris of our destructive trail. Now, I suppose, it is turning saline, poisoned like so much of that farmland by the most exhaustive agriculture in the world.

Then I began nightwork. Ploughing by headlights in such huge spaces is a hallucinatory occupation, with nothing but a small patch of light ahead of you, field mice scampering along the furrow and a cloud of dancing moths. I rapidly lost all sense of direction, blindly following the furrow, ploughing around rocks or stumps or crashing over them, freezing, choked by dust or clammy with damp in the cold morning dew, conscious only of the tractor's howl and, in occasional silences, the croak of frogs from the salt soaks. Many a night I ploughed to the centre of my patch and was unable to find my way out again, having to wait for dawn before moving on to the next section of the field. Once the plough was caught on a buried tree stump and within seconds the tractor sank over its axles – a shower of rain had turned the light soil to quicksand. There was no cab on the tractor, so for twelve hours each night I bucked and swayed in the cold air and anyone within earshot would have thought I was mad – I sang songs to keep awake and told myself funny stories, laughing at the punch lines, and dreamt of warm idle days on palm-fringed beaches. Once, to my delight, I happened to be working near the boundary of a neighbouring farm owned by an Italian immigrant and I realized that he, too, sang as he ploughed. Unlike me, he sang in tune.

When the ploughing was finished and we started seeding, I was glad to revert to day work. But accidents continued to enliven the monotony of the job. One day the steering of the tractor went suddenly mad – the wheel whipped round, nearly breaking my thumb, and the tractor spun in eccentric circles before heading for a pile of rocks. Since none of O'Dea's machines had brakes which worked, it was a matter of disengaging gear and hoping for the best. The same problem, absence of brakes, caused two other crises, both potentially lethal. I was following him home one day, driving an old truck with a seat so low that I could hardly see through the windscreen. We came down the only hill for miles, to the only crossroads, and O'Dea slowed, habitually brakeless, to a halt. I put my foot on the brakes. Nothing. I pulled on the handbrake – it flew upwards, tensionless, ineffective. Gathering momentum down the hill, I swerved past his stationary car, careered across the main road, up a bank and safely to rest in a field. Shaken, furious, I emerged demanding explanations. He seemed surprised. It was cheaper to coast to a stop than to maintain the brakes.

I learnt to cope but there were always difficulties. How do you hitch a tractor to a plough, singlehanded, unless you can back the tractor to the plough, apply the handbrake, step to the ground and wrestle with the connections? No problem, if both are on level ground, but on the slightest slope the tractor, brakeless, will slide away from (or into) the stationary plough. The answer was to get down, stand between both bits of equipment and ease the tractor back, operating the clutch lever with one hand (as gently as for a precipitous hill start) while lifting the plough linkage in the other and holding the link pin in your teeth. I became expert at coordinating these movements, aligning the connections and dropping the pin into the slot – until the day came when the clutch grabbled, the tractor roared backwards and I was caught in the middle as it smashed into the plough. Metal screamed and bended. I thought I was done for but somehow found a tiny space in the midst of this collision and survived, uncrushed, unbroken, just slightly bruised.

A week or two later, driving in a dream on a hot day, dazed by the sun and dust, I was blasted into attention by an explosion near the right wheel. For a wild moment, it seemed like a landmine. It was probably a live cartridge, dropped by a careless fox shooter, ignited by the tractor's weight.

A new rake arrived, with spiked six foot discs mounted on a mighty steel beam, as long as a bus. It was designed to rake up rocks and tree stumps on recently cleared land, aligning them in neat windrows like a hayrake, but it proved a difficult monster to steer. As it trailed at an angle behind the tractor, I found its rear end heading towards a spinney. Expecting catastrophe, the destruction of another expensive piece of equipment, I was relieved to see the young trees tumble like grass before a scythe.

Everything seemed on an epic scale. There was a sandstorm, with biting yellow dust roaring and swirling across the fields, whipped by the wind, seeping through the cracks of the Landrover where I had taken shelter. A week later it began to rain, deluging down to soak us with the wettest June in forty years. While the land dried out we were given 'odd jobs', to fill in time. Two of us erected twenty-one miles of fencing in four days (every post accurate to within an inch) and four of us tailed five hundred lambs in a couple of hours.

Then I went north, to find the emu-proof fence stretched across Western Australia, dividing the country between the thousand acre fields of the great agricultural plains and the ten thousand acre paddocks of the cattle ranches. Its purpose is to ban from the wheat fields those strange, scrawny and innocently destructive birds, whose large feet wreak havoc on the freshly sown land. There were plenty of them, supercilious but slightly ridiculous, chasing through the bush beside the road to Payne's Find, relic of Gold Rush days, where a few crazed miners sifted the debris of long-exhausted seams. Living like tramps, they still had a mad spark of adventure, the gambler's optimism. Searching for nuggets of gold, they also clubbed together to buy lottery tickets. One day, to everyone's surprise, their number came up. The most presentable member of the little band was sent down to Perth to collect the money while the rest planned a party. Weeks went by and eventually the prodigal returned, penniless. He had spent all the winnings on a mighty bender, on drink and on girls. None of them resented it – they knew that each would have done the same – and they revelled by proxy in the tales of his extravagance. In their broken-down, hobo way, these crazy old men preserved the dreams of the pioneers.

Such dreams have long been forgotten, south of the Fence. There was a time when stockmen from the northern ranches made epic journeys, herding thousands of cattle down the trail from waterhole to distant waterhole, weeks on the journey to bring their beasts to market. Teams of twenty oxen drew lumbering carts to the railhead, laden with great bales of wool. Camel trains crossed the great Australian deserts, tended by Persian drovers. These memories seem like a mirage in a land where they round up the herds by aeroplane. Farming has become industrialized. Exploration ended; isolated on their enormous farms, miles from the nearest neighbour, the imagination of these farmers is starved of sustenance. There is, instead, a claustrophobic meanness of spirit which spills over into occasional acts of bravado but is most evidently manifest in the slowly poisoned land.

A couple of crazy brothers, annoyed at the cawing of the galahs around their house, caught one, tied a stick of dynamite to its body and lit the fuse. They hoped it would fly back up to the flock but the bird had its revenge. Weighed down by Nobel's legacy, it flapped along at head height, pursuing the terrified brothers across two fields, and exploded just as they leapt for the safety of a ditch. Other farmers, equally reckless, fly home drunk and crash their planes into the hills or trees.

Geoff O'Dea, my first employer, had no such vices but he was notorious for his parsimony, even in a region of tight-fisted millionaires. His only extravagance was to buy the biggest, most expensive agricultural equipment which he would abandon after a season's use in the distant corners of his thirteen thousand acre farm. Rusting tractors would lie forgotten until cannibalized for spare parts. O'Dea never smoked or drank or swore, never took a holiday, but spent his days in tense soliloquies, shuffling the permutations of the week's work and brooding on the probability of ruin. Living like a pauper, stingy even with words, he was a hard man to work for and I was glad to leave. Towards the end I grew accustomed to his terse ways, almost got to like him, but I couldn't stand the food.

He believed in living off the farm, which meant sheep every day: a chop with my breakfast egg, cold mutton sandwiches for lunch, an over-roasted joint in the evening. It was worse when I worked the night shift – 'Mother' O'Dea served their re-heated supper when I returned home at seven in the morning.

I was offered a job by Jim Moorhouse, recently arrived from Huddersfield. For two months I worked happily, not a sheep in sight, enjoying Yorkshire pudding on Sundays and the agreeable rhythms of a common culture. Then it was time to move on again, to the wealthiest farmer in the region. I soon found myself missing the familiar stinginess of O'Dea. My new employer seemed a grand fellow to all outward appearances, but he was a private bully, incomparably mean. And he fed his family on the oldest, sickest sheep in the flock, the stragglers, which he shot in the field, skinned and butchered in the yard. It was back to stale mutton, thrice daily.

Two phrases, two cultures. One evening I was out looking for a stray cow with Jim Moorhouse. As we passed a small wood he stopped, peered and moved sadly on. 'I thought I'd seen a white face, but it was only the grass through the trees.' A fortnight later, the millionaire reached for his rifle and headed for the paddock in search of supplies. 'Just going to shoot a sheep for breakfast.'

I jumped in the car and drove across the continent, heading for Sydney, racing to the sea.

Bulcamp Lamb

Wrap a medium-sized leg of best lamb in masses of fresh rosemary (tying the bundle with string) and roast in a hot oven for twelve minutes per pound.

Remove from oven and discard rosemary. Allow to cool until you can handle the warm meat comfortably and then use the fingers (with a little assistance from a sharp knife) to separate the part-roast leg into several sections of different size, following the seams of the muscles. This may sound complicated but is easy once you start. Discard the bones and trim the meat to remove any fat.

Sprinkle with a little salt, black pepper and dried thyme and grill over charcoal or the hot embers of a wood fire, until sealed and brown without, pink within. Carve into thick slices. Serve with a squeeze of lemon, spinach and devilled spuds, or with a purée of winter vegetables (carrots, leeks and turnips).

Suggested Wine In summer the claret or Teroldego mentioned for the previous recipe. In winter a top-quality Châteauneuf-du-Pape, from Château de Beaucastel or Domaine du Vieux Télégraphe.

SATURDAY NIGHT AT THE
MOVIES

I am sitting at OG's in the Village with a glass of Grolsch, when in comes Bob Gale to announce that his friend, Henry Nielson, is boxing his first professional match that night out at Long Island Stadium. Seeing my lack of enthusiasm, he promises a ride out in a classic old convertible.

The car is a dream, a big early-sixties sprawl of grey fins and chrome with red seats and the hood folded back, a cruiser, and that evening the radio stations are all playing golden oldies. We climb in the back, Bob, Jane and myself, and I shake hands with the driver – broken nose, face out of an early Brando movie. 'Hi Henry, nice to meet you.' 'My name's Roy. Henry's just gone to pick up his wife Jennifer and they've lost the boxing permit.'

When Henry arrives he doesn't look much like a fighter, being fairly undamaged and not noticeably musclebound. He wants to be a sports journalist and is fighting professionally in order to accumulate some credentials. Jennifer is rich and somewhat distracted at the prospect of her man getting pulped by Dancing Kid Carlos from Puerto Rico who has been boxing with fair success for the past five years.

We drive out towards Long Island, the radio playing and Jennifer cuddling Henry, whispering into his ear, stroking his hair, hyping him up for the fight. Behind us the towers of Manhattan gleam in the sunset and as dusk comes we cruise through the wastelands, past the surburban shacks and the scrapyards, sailing along the freeway with Chuck Berry lost in the slipstream of the open car.

Long Island Stadium is large, concrete and ugly, standing in the middle of a vast empty parking lot. Inside it smells of sweat and popcorn and the empty echoing spaces are nicely calculated to demoralize a young boxer facing his first professional fight. Henry disappears to change and perform whatever mental rituals are necessary to prepare himself for battle. The rest of us gather round the hot dog counter as we wait for the bar to open.

Slowly come the crowds – first the old professionals of the fight game, the fixers, the managers, the hangers-on, a couple of reporters from the sporting press – then the public, families out for an evening of blood and drama. Jennifer hits the whisky and the conversation gets a little manic, nobody quite willing to express their panic certainty that Henry's going to get beaten. There is now a respectable crowd around the ring at the centre of this huge stadium; most of them, it seems, the family and friends of Carlos who has arrived looking very cocky, strutting around like a matador in a tight powder-blue jumpsuit with a banana stuffed down his pants, Speedy Gonzalez himself, with his girl looking very fine and proud of her man. His grin is engaging and his entourage intimidating. We knock off a few more whiskies.

By this stage I am drunk enough to be interested in the entertainment and we grab seats as the pretzel sellers begin working the crowd. A couple of pretzels to anchor the whisky and the buzz mounts. The judges, old weighty men, seat themselves with some importance and chew on fat cigars as the referee confers with the MC, strangled by his thin bow tie, and suddenly the lights above the ring brighten and My God it's Henry and Carlos to fight first and here comes Henry looking *dreadful*, white and puny beneath a gaudy dressing gown proclaiming him the South Carolina Champ in gleaming yellow and blue satin. Carlos is clearly the favourite, shorter than Henry but looking very fit and confident, dancing and shadow boxing in his corner while Henry confers with his trainer.

The bell goes and Carlos comes out fast as his family roars and Jennifer, pale and drunk, starts screaming for her man. For the first couple of rounds things look bad, but Henry survives and our cheering grows more confident. He's also beginning to attract disinterested support, and as he moves onto the offensive the crowd realizes that the contest has begun to change character, with the more thoughtful fighter gaining the space he needs to operate and Carlos increasingly finding himself striking air. Henry connects a couple of punches that hurt and suddenly we find ourselves shouting for Nielson and the crowd around us join in as we cheer him through the last round and the fight is his and the rest of the evening looks bearable because the final bell goes and Henry has won.

The prospect of the event had evoked no more than a fatalistic curiosity but the fight itself generated a response which combined partisan interest, the excitement of violence by proxy and the gambler's exhilaration at his horse coming home by a head. Henry had a theory that the fighter could transcend the ugly brutality of his profession if he pursued a technical victory, using his opponent's strength and momentum to make his blows count and to preserve his pretty face. His scheme worked but the fight which had the whole crowd on its feet, cheering and shouting (myself included) was not his conceptual, non-violent approach but the exuberant, joyful, dancing ferocity with which the forty-eight-year-old Emperor Hilton, supposedly a sheep for the slaughter, punched the morose young heavyweight challenger clean through the ropes into the laps of his disconsolate comforters. The fixers, aiming to record another win for their investment, sulked, but we cheered the old black in his victory dance.

This was the essence of Hollywood, real life conforming to its stereotypes, and everyone knew their parts. Henry's triumph was eclipsed by this epic, leaving Jennifer less convincing and certainly less convinced in the rôle of prizefighter's moll that she had caught so well on the drive to the stadium. The lines came less fluently and eventually she changed to another script, the manic rich girl, drunk and sophisticated, vamping the other men as she mocks her sullen hunk of muscle – a cruel rôle that she played with relish, uninhibited by the miscasting of Henry as the hulk.

It was late and we were all extremely hungry, so we stopped on the way back into New York at Caesar's Hostellerie, a roadhouse in three acts. The menu was the same throughout, but you could choose to sit in the Western Saloon, the English Tavern or the Grecian Room, every detail of the original television sets for these period dramas being lovingly reproduced in plastic. The food had an equally cinematic quality: 'farmfresh and wholesome', the bacon and eggs looked superb but had neither texture nor taste. The absence of alcoholic beverages might have damaged the visual credibility on set but the designers had solved that problem by serving the coffee in period pottery wine goblets. Working on the assumption that showgirls are interchangeable in any epoch, the waitresses tottered between sets in high heels and fishnet stockings.

The whole of American history, the ideals of American ethics and the prototypes of the American family, the American dream and the American God were all invented in Hollywood. That seems to me entirely reasonable.

What I cannot forgive the celluloid moguls is that they also invented American food.

Bagels

Fresh bagels, cream cheese and smoked salmon form a combination of luxurious simplicity, irresistible to adults and children. It's the next best thing to being in New York.

Suggested Wine Neat, ice-cold Danish Akvavit is perfect with smoked salmon, but dangerous fuel for a party. The alternatives are Champagne, or Guinness (but *not* a mixture of the two) or Bourgogne Aligoté de Bouzeron, from Aubert de Villaine – a lovely, characterful example of this sometimes difficult grape.

WHITE RIVER CATFISH

One evening in New York, in a cramped and cluttered office on the thirtieth floor of the Time Life Building, I watched a perfect sunset across a desk littered with yellow memo forms. Silhouetted against the dramatic sky, incongruous in that landscape of steel and glass, were numerous small wooden towers with conical roofs, perched on stilts on the top of apartment blocks. In the following days I noticed them everywhere, relics of the nineteenth century washed up by some mysterious current onto the towers of Manhattan: normal stratification reversed; the old piled on the new. Perhaps the urge to rebuild, to obliterate the past, ran out as the buildings rose higher. By the time they reached the top, nostalgia had reasserted itself. Whatever the reason, it was exhilarating to discover that there are still families whose craft is to build and repair these wooden cisterns, using the ancient skills of the cooper to maintain water pressure in the apartments of psychiatrists.

I expected to discover the culinary equivalents of these water tanks, gastronomic memories of an earlier age, but they are rare. Jewish traditions have survived better than most (begels and blintzés being ideal convenience foods), but there is a reduction of national tradition to simple travesty. Italy is represented by the pizza, Germany the hamburger and France, cruelly, by french fries. The roast beef of England has been simplified to steak, while the main legacy of the Irish seems to be a contempt for all vegetables except the onion and the potato.

New Yorkers, in any case, eat the décor: their choice of restaurant has little to do with the food. They go because the waiters insult them (a sign of privileged intimacy), because they like eating in a conservatory filled with palm trees or because of the other customers. It's an even bet that the more expensive the setting and the more verbose the menu, the worse the food, but at least you can enjoy the show. A great deal of fun can be had from eavesdropping in fashionable corners.

Ensconced at an expensive table in Mortimer's, I listened with fascination to the indiscretions of rich and glamorous women, fresh from a couple of hours with hairdresser or manicurist, discussing each other's lovers and facelifts. The waiters wore the long white aprons of smart Dublin barmen and served their clientele with a similar distracted inefficiency. The quality of the food reinforced the Irish atmosphere. At the bar, two grooms from the racetrack of Long Island (straw in their hair and Guinness at their elbows) discussed horses and form with Beamish, the greeter, while my host rambled on about the Stud Book. It took me a while to realize that he was referring to the Social Register.

Surfeited with gossip, I longed for somewhere to eat that was simple, old-fashioned and unpretentious. The Oyster Bar at Grand Central Station had just been re-decorated, losing its comfortable, well-worn appeal, so I settled instead for Mary Elizabeth's. Situated a few blocks from the Empire State Building, frequented by diet-conscious ladies in the rag trade, it presents an intriguing contrast to downtown Manhattan. It is staffed by retired nannies and its dark interior is seemingly unchanged since 1910. When Eva from Lancashire takes your order for a pot of tea, you realize that the last outpost of Empire flourishes on East 37th Street.

The English retain few such bastions and their appeal is nostalgic, not gastronomic, but the Italians and Chinese are everywhere. This raises the spirits of the hungry traveller, only to dash them on the rocks of expatriate reality: immigrants from Naples or Sicily are not proficient at making the wonderful dishes of north Italy and the Chinese (other than those outgoing countrymen from Szechuan) keep their best cooking to themselves. There are few more daunting experiences than eating in the Silver Palace Restaurant, in Chinatown. Surrounded by a thousand Chinese families, at hundreds of closely packed tables, you struggle for attention and are given a small typewritten translation of the menu that lists less than one in ten of the dishes actually available. It is in any case irrelevant since the food is served from trollies, hauled in endless circles around the vast room. As they passed, I would grab whatever unidentifiable delicacies seemed most appealing, a chancy business that led to bizarre combinations of taste succeeding each other with great rapidity. Green tea acted as a balm to the stomach, but could not raise a sinking heart, oppressed by the unfriendliness, the food and the bill, which was calculated by some arcane computation of the number, colour and shape of the empty dishes piled on the table.

It seemed difficult to discover in Manhattan anywhere (however exalted) that didn't suffer from the fast food imperatives of appearance and convenience. I wanted something earthier.

My chance came when I started to plan a trip across the continent and met Calvin Trillin. His enthusiasm for good food extends to the most unlikely places and has spilled out of his bulging files of references and recommendations into a couple of wonderfully entertaining books and numerous columns in the *New Yorker*. We pored over a map as he and Alice planned my route from a log cabin in Virginia to Brother Jack's in Knoxville, the Camel East in Memphis and Fisher's Barbecue in Little Rock. 'You have to visit the Indian pueblo at Taos,' said Alice. 'And there's a great Mexican restaurant in Española where you can have lunch,' said he. As they organized my schedule, from breakfast to dinner, there seemed to be a gap in Arkansas. Out of Trillin's files came a note that someone had telephoned him in the middle of the night in an attempt to persuade him to fly out from New York to eat at Murry's Cafe in DeVall's Bluff. 'It has to be the greatest catfish restaurant in the world.'

The countryside of Pennsylvania and Virginia seemed suffused with nostalgia, whether because of the Amish, who stopped the clock at the turn of the century, or the sight of those lovingly restored colonial houses, pillared and portico'd, surrounded by fine trees, lush grass and the scent of honeysuckle.

As I followed the Appalachian mountains south, the landscape grew wilder, then more barren, and lost altogether the green, gentlemanly feel of the old estates.

In Knoxville, Tennessee, I eventually found Brother Jack's in a somewhat ramshackle part of town, advertised by no other sign than the stark announcement 'Fresh Meat'. A couple of posts held up the roof and a shelf ran along the back wall, just wide enough to place a glass on. Behind the counter loomed a tall, rather faded black man with a lugubrious smile, Brother Jack. What did he have to offer? Pork, said he, and went to fetch it. As he carved a few slices he explained that the shoulder of pork had been impregnated with his secret concoction of spices and barbecued over a very slow fire for twenty four hours. It smelt delicious.

He urged us to try his homemade sauce, hot or hotter. I took up the challenge and was just beginning to wonder what all the fuss was about when a bomb went off at the back of my throat. Groping for a glass of water, I saw Brother Jack casually stuffing a handful of fresh red chillies into his mouth.

'Y'know how old Ah am? Seventy four. Ah open this place at ten in the morning an' Ah don't close till three the next morning. Then Ah clear up, go home an' have breakfast an' Ah sleep from six to eight. An' Ah eat plenty of chillies. Don't you feel nice an' fresh after that sauce?'

Tears streaming down my face and sweat dripping from my brow, I bowed to a hero.

Hundreds of miles later, drifting down towards the south, we arrived in the wide, fertile, waterlogged land of the Mississippi valley. Small, dilapidated clapboard houses stood under cottonwood trees, isolated in flat fields under the vast sky, with piles of trash and new pick-up trucks parked outside. The freeway from Knoxville to Little Rock cut the landscape from horizon to horizon. We turned left, wandered for six miles down narrow lanes past isolated homesteads sleeping in the heavy, humid afternoon, and arrived at a street lined with small wooden houses, shady trees, honeysuckle and rambling creepers. This is sitting-on-the-porch country. An old man, half blind, was rocking on a rickety chair, spooning cold beans from a small pan. His house was that indeterminate grey which could have been unpainted clapboard dried silver or paint which had cracked, softened and weathered through the years of hot summers and sudden storms. The wooden frame had twisted slightly at every joint like the old man, dried and warped with age. A large cottonwood shaded the scene, dark trunk and branches seen through the bright green of spring foliage over the darker green of lush, damp grass sloping to a shallow ditch beside the road.

The old man told of his troubles in a cracked, meditative voice – cataracts in both eyes, wife in hospital, children long gone to distant cities. 'And where you from, son?' 'England.' 'That England, Arkansas?' Aah!, Middle America. How do you explain geography to a man for whom England is a seldom-visited town, a few miles away? The Atlantic Ocean lies nine hundred miles to the east. I mentioned London and recognition flickered. 'Guess you do have a kinda funny accent. Ah thought maybe you was a relative of ma cousin Wilbur. Y'unerstan ah can't see too good.'

DeVall's Bluff, population 622. 'Not the half of that, I do believe, not less everybody got relatives visitin.' Thus the cheerful comment of the only man in sight when I stopped to ask directions. Being both black and fat he had to know the way and, sure enough, a beatific smile spread across his face at the mention of Murry's. 'You go down that dirt track an cross the railway. Then it gets kinda rough an you gover the plank bridge an turn left when you hit the blacktop. An Murry, he's up there on the left.'

The Corvette that I was delivering to Los Angeles had two-inch clearance and was no car for exploring the byways. Scraping and crunching at two miles an hour we finally made it to the blacktop. The hedgerows dripped with honeysuckle and in the languorous stillness of the late afternoon the damp air was heavy with its scent. On the left, in a clearing by the road, a couple of low trailers were pulled together beside a small house outside which an old black man with a cook's apron was sitting in the

sun. Around him ran a boy of four or five, long dread-
locks and a big grin. 'This Murry's?' 'Sure is,' said the old
man as he hitched himself off his stool and led us up a
couple of steps into the front trailer – half a dozen tables,
bench seats and the smell of good cooking from the
kitchen out the back. 'Got any catfish?', I asked the most
famous catfish cook in America. Murry, for it was he,
smiled quietly. 'Sure do,' he said, turning towards the
kitchen.

Stanley, father of the boy with the big grin, gave us the
menus. On the red cover were the words 'Murry's Cafe'
above an old fashioned drawing of a whiskery fish and
the subtitle 'White River Catfish'. The list of specialities
(Crappie Dinner, Fried Quail Dinner, Steak and Tails,
Frog Leg Dinner) was headed by the Jumbo Catfish
Dinner ($5), the Regular Catfish Dinner ($4.50) and the
One Half Catfish Dinner ($3.75).

Hey, we came here to eat a fish course before visiting
Fisher's Barbecue at Little Rock. Stanley suggested the
Half Catfish Dinner. Any beer? 'No, we ain't licensed to
sell liquor but ah feel kinda thirsty myself so if you folks
wanna ride along with me, we c'n drive down to the store
and get ourselves a couple of sixpacks.'

Stanley, Stanley Jnr, Jane and I piled into his pick-up
and headed off to the store with Stanley laughing at Jesse
telling us to come by the dirt road and the plank bridge
when we coulda saved ourselves a lot of aggravation by
going the way we'se goin now, and was pretty pleased to
hear about the fame of Murry's spreading as far as New
York and that we had come all the way from England,
Europe. 'The old man was cook on the riverboats all his
life 'til about twelve year ago when he started his own
place. Sure is famous for catfish round here. Yessir.' And
he wrestled the wheel from Stanley Jnr who wanted to

drive the pick-up. We grabbed a couple of sixpacks at the general store, were introduced as friends from England, and Stanley was ripping the top off his first can as we climbed back into the truck. Almost as fast, I prized the cap off my bottle with the door hinge. 'You bin practisin?' said Stanley.

As we stepped back into the restaurant, our Half Catfish Dinners were laid on the table. Huge plates were piled with catfish. Covered in Murry's mixture of meal, breadcrumbs, eggs and seasonings, it was fried crisp outside, white and moist within. There were Hush Puppies (golden cornmeal cakes), Murry's wonderful coleslaw and french fries (like no others that I've ever had), and wedges of lemon and small, sweet, green peppers. Ecstacy, after the plastic menus of motel restaurants; food that made you hungry looking at it.

The place had filled up a bit since we left to get the beer. Three middle-aged white ladies had come in from having their hair done to have a glass of iced tea and a chat with Murry. A man from Little Rock was tucking into a Regular Catfish Dinner before driving home with one 'to go' in case he felt peckish at the end of the journey. He claimed there were half a dozen catfish restaurants in Little Rock but none to compare with Murry's and boasted that he made the three hundred and fifty mile round trip two or three times a month. Stanley settled down for another beer, murmuring 'Yep. Those folks comes here all the way from London, England.'

It was peaceful and friendly, sitting there eating catfish and drinking beer and listening to the slow, lazy drawl of the Mississippi flatlands and the bustle in the kitchen at the back as they prepared for the evening rush.

We left in a sudden thunderstorm. Within minutes the land was flooded and the roads were torrents. As we passed the blind man, still sitting on the porch of his old grey house under the big cottonwood, I tuned the car radio through bands of static. FM104 was the station Stanley had recommended.

Catfish

You are unlikely to find Mississippi catfish at the local fishmonger but occasionally he may have the sea-going variety – another whiskery creature, despised by most customers because of its name.

The flesh is fairly firm-textured, and can be slightly coarse, but is good if cooked gently in the oven on a julienne of carrots and leeks, moistened with a little fish stock. It can be served with a lightly curried sauce.

Alternatively, marinate briefly in lemon juice and dip bite-sized chunks in a sieved mixture of flour and curry powder. Sauté until golden on both sides in a little olive oil. Serve with Greek sheep's yoghurt, mixed with chopped fennel leaves or young sorrel.

Suggested Wine Favorita is a little-known Italian grape variety, a speciality of Piedmont, which reminds me of fresh pears, with a lively, succulent, springlike acidity. The best, almost the only version comes from Roberto Damonte. Since this is almost as hard to find as fresh catfish, I proffer as an alternative the Viognier grape, from the Rhône. There are several expensive Condrieus made from this variety (plus Château Grillet) but an interesting alternative is produced further south, by Domaine St Anne. Like Favorita, these wines must be drunk young.

CASINO CUISINE:
TESTING THE RITZ

From Alunite it is downhill all the way, twenty miles in a dead straight line to the centre of the desert, encircled by distant mountains. Airliners descend through the clear sky, reflecting the sun, and then vanish into the haze which hangs above Las Vegas, American Gomorrah, city of the plain. There is fire in the air and it seems that brimstone has been rained upon the ground, for the atmosphere is veiled with the fumes of sulphur.

As you approach, Las Vegas loses this lurid tinge and looks merely tacky, a parking lot littered with the remnants of a thousand film sets. It is hard to understand what curious process of evolution should have transformed the original Mormon settlement into this living soap opera, city of marriage parlours and slot machines. Pulling levers and pushing buttons, the crowd stands shoulder to shoulder, each sad face intent, oblivious, alone. And there is the noise, the constant, inescapable twenty-four hour sound of machines eating money.

In the midst of the mechanical payoff and the plastic glitter, six men were playing poker. This was the real thing, five card stud, for enormous stakes. The dense huddle of speculators was almost silent, absorbed by the drama, watching the last game of the World Championship.

A few days earlier, the top poker players from around the world had gathered in Las Vegas, each bringing his entry stake of ten thousand dollars. The rules were simple, winner takes all. These were the survivors.

The casting director had done a perfect job. There was the small-town judge out of a western movie (white goatee beard, black frock coat, satin-faced waistcoat, string tie). One hand held a cheroot and the other fidgeted with his watch chain. A tall Texan from Dallas complete with silk suit, Stetson and heavily tooled boots, leaned back in his chair and called for a drink, watching his opponents with a smile. The man from LA, very cool in cream suit and open-necked shirt, basked in the admiration of his girlfriend. A heavy-set mid-westerner, in lumberjack's checked shirt, made a lot of noise, cracking jokes with the audience as he raised the stakes. He had the crumpled face of a drunkard. With his back to me was the youngest player, a New Yorker; thin, middle height, white shirt and jeans, still as a snake. Only his eyes flickered, like the snake's tongue, ready to strike. The sixth man was the dealer, a quiet professional.

For a while the stacks of chips moved backwards and forwards across the table without much evident change in fortune, but checked shirt's pile was being steadily eroded. He went for the big pot and lost to the Texan. Cleaned out. There was a brief hubbub of excited gossip. Then the Californian made the running with a series of modest wins but the other three began to stake big money and suddenly he, too, was on the sidelines, being consoled by his girl and a bottle of Dom Perignon. There was a long period of stalemate and I went to get a drink. When I returned the Texan was out of the game and the atmosphere was electric.

The judge still sat there with his cheroot, smiling

through the smoke, but he no longer looked like an amiable fake. He was well ahead, with an enormous pile of chips in front of him. The New Yorker remained utterly expressionless and quietly won the next two hands. They were back on even terms.

A new pack of cards was shuffled and dealt. The betting opened with the New Yorker showing a pair of twos, the judge a king and a ten. Suddenly it was clear that this was the final hand. The pot grew steadily bigger. Then the New Yorker pushed the rest of his chips to the centre and, after a brief pause, the judge matched him. All the money was on the table.

They flicked over the cards. The judge had another king, a six and a two. There was a collective sigh; experience, it seemed, had won. But the New Yorker was smiling for the first time that night. As his hand was revealed the crowd gasped. There, unbelievably, was the remaining two.

He walked away from the game with eight hundred thousand dollars and asked for a BLT.

The bacon, lettuce and tomato sandwich might not have featured in the Hollywood re-make of this gambling epic, but it seemed a great idea to me. Abrupt hunger after intense concentration demands a delicious snack not a meal, especially in the middle of the night. It seemed a neglected area of culinary research. I began to consider casino cuisine.

Las Vegas is no place to start – the food is appalling – but those were the days when London was the gambling capital of Europe and the casinos vied with one another to attract wealthy punters, offering every sort of inducement (legal and illegal) which led eventually to many of them being closed. It was paradise for gourmet gamblers; the casinos employed the best chefs in town.

I helped to organize a tasting of eighteen vintages of Château Petrus (back to 1945) which was hosted by Craig Dent, then catering manager at the Curzon House Club. He had tremendous ideas for midnight eating: 'A brochette of scallops and bacon with a salad of lamb's lettuce; or the thinnest pancake, made with a savagely beaten egg, filled with sour cream and dill.' But he had to admit that few of his customers paid any attention. Offered a free meal, they opted for asparagus and lobster (or a steak), even at three o'clock in the morning.

The Curzon House (now Aspinall's) still has the highest reputation for its food but other casinos frankly admit to the problems. 'We have the best menu in London but all they want to eat is steak and chips or a hamburger,' wails the girl from The Ritz Casino, while at Crockford's the biggest demand is for falafel and spring rolls. Such food, however well cooked, must surely dull the brain. Nighthawks and gamblers would be better advised to imitate Joe Dwek, London's most successful backgammon player, and stick to Florentine eggs.

My own preference is for Bacon du Bedat. Invented by Bill du Bedat, refined by Victor Gordon, this is the perfect combination of smoked salmon, bacon and chutney, sandwiched between lightly toasted white bread. Extremely difficult to serve correctly (toast warm, bacon hot, smoked salmon cold) it is the ultimate challenge to a distant kitchen.

I took my wife and daughter to tea in the Palm Court at The Ritz and calmly ordered Bacon du Bedat sandwiches for three. The waiter, of course, had never heard of any such thing, but politely asked for an explanation and retired to discuss it with the chef. Eventually he returned, with a limp attempt at this blissful concoction, all the ingredients uniformly lukewarm. I sent it back. Somewhere in the depths I could hear the wailing and gnashing of teeth. Then the waiter reappeared, gravely carrying a tray.

On the tray was a spirit stove, keeping warm a chafing dish of perfectly cooked bacon; a plate of smoked salmon, sitting on a bowl of ice; a bowl of mango chutney and several slices of toast, wrapped in a napkin. He assembled the ingredients before our eyes and, with a modest air of triumph, presented the perfect result. Bravo, Bravissimo.

Acknowledging our applause, he reminded me for a moment of that New Yorker in Las Vegas, when they turned over his cards to reveal, beside his modest pair, the critical two of spades.

Bacon du Bedat

The present form of this recipe is the invention of Victor Gordon. As already mentioned, the sandwich consists of good quality white bread, thinly sliced and lightly toasted, enclosing smoked salmon, bacon, mango chutney and (according to Victor, though I have my doubts about this) some pickle. Not as easy as it sounds, but more economical, you can use smoked salmon scraps (often available quite cheaply from the fishmonger).

Cook the bacon and keep warm. Make the toast. Lay cold smoked salmon on warm toast, spread with chutney/pickle, add hot bacon and final layer of toast and eat *at once*. A minute or two's delay ruins the effect.

Suggested Wine Traditionally this is eaten with Champagne, the grander the better. Gamblers may prefer coffee.

ROOM WITH A VIEW

There is a poem by Lorca about the death of a matador, gored in the bullring at five in the afternoon. That refrain 'a las cinqo de la tarde', echoes through the poem and sticks in the mind. It's such a banal time to die, one of those sluggish moments in the day which remind me of low tide on the mudflats; an in-between stillness before the air is refreshed by the returning current and the heat of the day softens into the balmy shadows of a summer evening, filled with expectation.

Times like these, the unfashionable pauses between events, are the moments to install yourself in the bars and cafés, to sit in the corner and watch. Addicts of invisibility soon become expert. By eleven thirty in the morning the bartenders should have finished counting the bottles and stocking the shelves, and have recovered from the uncertain moods of breakfast. You can choose the best table from which to observe the world, settle yourself with a newspaper and wait for the coffee or dry martini which starts the day. They will serve you efficiently, undistracted by other customers, with the restful, half-attentive air that they apply to the habitual tasks of their morning routine, before the rush. After a week or two you don't even need to speak – they will bring your drink with the same professional rhythm that they polish the glasses or feed the parrot.

As the place fills up you remain invisible, part of the furniture. Groups of friends come in, chattering loudly, and individuals, looking around for the lover or client or agent whom they have arranged to meet. It is fun to speculate on relationships. There are eddies and whorls as the crowd breaks and reforms into differing clusters, the floaters drifting between those who establish a focus by remaining still. The noise level rises. The barmen work faster, swapping gossip with the regulars.

This is an urban pleasure, dependent on anonymity, and can be enjoyed in most cities. It is also one of the best ways of letting the character of a place seep into your awareness.

The brown bars of Amsterdam are the perfect spots to observe a neighbourhood, especially on a quiet Sunday morning. Lingering over a late breakfast and a glass of Dutch gin, you can sense the peaceful, domestic character of the city with canals modifying sound and light, and listen to the lively but restful sounds of Dutch conversation. A child is doing his homework in the corner, a girl reads the newspaper over a cup of coffee, and a miscellaneous group of local friends gathers for a drink before lunch. There is a domestic scale, seemingly little changed from the days of Pieter de Hoogh.

It is utterly different from the crowded, noisy, cosmopolitan entertainment which can be enjoyed from a corner of Harry's Bar in Venice. The characters are more dramatic. There is an enigmatic face, old, mask-like and beautiful, unmistakably Italian, elusively familiar. She acknowledges your recognition, though you have never met. An old-fashioned, civilized American accent draws your attention to the elderly couple in the corner. They

are talking with an English dealer, gossiping about
mutual friends and the intrigues of the art market in the
same agreeable tone of voice that they discuss the difference between muffins and crumpets. A tempestuously
beautiful girl is whispering to her companion, a drama
that erupts in her sudden departure. In many ways the
most intriguing to watch are the waiters, endlessly re-
arranging the tiny space, wheeling in table tops, taking
out chairs and serving the ever-changing clientele with a
flourish of professional pride and individual bravado.
Each is a character, with alive Italian faces that somehow
seem rather dated, like the place itself, a witty evocation
of the thirties.

Most peculiarly Venetian is its location; the secretive
narrow door in a dark alley, a few paces from the mouth
of the Grand Canal, with the words Harry's Bar dis-
creetly etched on the glass.

There could hardly be a greater contrast than La
Coupole in Paris, largest of the great café restaurants, but
here again much of the pleasure is in watching professionals at work. There are subtle rankings of precedence
and function, a rigid hierarchy amongst the cohorts of
waiters as they jostle for succession to the best positions,
in the centre of the room, where the weekly tips are said
to be enormous. Ushering new arrivals to a table, taking
an order, beckoning to a minion or serving a plate of
oysters, these are characters from Daumier or Lautrec.

Equally intriguing is the clientele, for La Coupole is far
too big to be the haunt of any particular coterie – it serves
a cross-section of Parisian life. There are families eating
together, three generations celebrating an anniversary.
Flamboyantly dressed eccentrics parade by the bar,
arguing about the cinema, and timid clerks sit at the outer
tables, with an omelette. There are solitary old men,

buried in *Le Monde*, and young men, writing; beautiful girls; intellectual tramps: a gallery of faces from every French movie. The pillars which divide the enormous room were painted in the thirties. by young artists in payment for their meals and have a period appeal, as does the menu which makes no concession to fashion but offers the reassurance of continuity.

This unchanging character of the place encourages, in its clients, a comparable conservatism. At La Coupole, for reasons which I cannot explain, I always order 'oeuf en gelée' and a glass of Polish vodka, followed by 'curry d'agneau'. Such habits have attached themselves to each of my favourite oases.

La Coupole is a good place to enjoy the range of Parisian life. For a more restricted view, perhaps one old man in a shaft of sunlight, I love the long bar at the Grand Theatre of Bordeaux. Almost nobody ever goes there but it is a wonderful classical room, gloomy and run down, with the sort of seedy grandeur which I find irresistible; faded gilt and marbled columns, roundels of tarnished clouds. It is a restful place, very tall, very long and very empty. At half past five on a hot July afternoon there is a man reading a newspaper with an empty cup of coffee in front of him, in the shadows towards the rear of the room, and a couple nearer the open doors, silhouetted against the sunshine and the traffic. She is sexy, of a certain age, with close-cropped dark hair and a bright summery dress riding up her thighs as she leans forward to laugh at the man, her lover. They chat comfortably, joking together as good friends. There is a thin gold chain around her brown ankle.

A shaggy dog wanders in from the bright pavements and lies down on the cool floor, panting. The waiter asks each of us if the dog is ours. No one owns him.

Room with a View

Under the colonnades of the Grand Theatre the streams of passers-by are oblivious – they never glance inside, never notice this oasis of antiquated peace. I have only once seen this bar full, during the interval of a memorably awful production of *Adrianna Lecouvreur*, when it seemed that all the dreams of Fellini had been emptied into the room at once. There was a ten-year-old boy, a pallid genius in enormous spectacles, wearing a blue sailor jacket, very long shorts and buckled shoes: a cross between Einstein On The Beach and Little Lord Fauntleroy. An adult version of the same confusion rubbed shoulders with a couple of Isadora Duncans, a female wrestler, two elegant priests and a very elegant bishop, Three Men in a Boat, various Heroes of the Resistance, several members of a pre-war Berlin revue and numerous red-faced penguins. There were also a couple of farmers, in overalls and berets, but I think it possible they had simply dropped in for a quiet drink, hence their appearance of stupefied shock. It was a re-markable demonstration of the effect of opera on a respectable provincial town.

On the whole my preference is for dramas which are less self-conscious than that fantastic parade at the Grand Theatre. I enjoy the small-scale spectacles of daily life. There was a grocer's in Waterford, for example, which had an inner room, approached through the shop past sacks of spuds and stacks of broom handles, where you could sit and drink a pint of stout or a glass of port and listen to the ticking of the old clock on the wall. This bar was like a private box at the theatre, with its view into the shop, and I could happily have spent hours there, listen-ing to the bell every time the street door opened, the sounds of gentle conversation as a solitary customer ordered a packet of tea and a few slices of ham; accumulating the fragments of gossip which I hate to be told but love to overhear.

There are corners like this all over the world, at every level of society; the lobby of Brown's Hotel in London or the Algonquin in New York, the tea shops of the Persian bazaars, the Eagle Cafe in San Francisco and the Market Cafe in Spitalfields. Best of all, there was Carrolls.

It's very hard to say why one salt beef bar in Soho should be infinitely more appealing than any other but Carrolls somehow was the one. I first went there with my father, when I was ten or twelve, and rediscovered it on my own a few years later. I never told anyone else about it but shortly after we met I took Irène there, only to find that she already knew it, was a regular.

Carrolls was in Windmill Street, up the pavement from another salt beef bar which I never entered. I liked the name, which seemed curiously Irish for so Jewish a place, and I liked the people. The owner, Mark, used to sit on a stool just inside the door, greeting his friends, and there were a couple of cheerful old men who carved the beef and used to shout the orders down to the kitchen through a speaking tube, eventually replaced by an intercom. Occasionally some figure would emerge from the depths, carrying a bowl of soup which would be served by the Italian waiter. Best of all, I liked the place itself.

The walls were painted a peaceful shade of pale green (the same faded turquoise as my favourite chai shop in Isfahan bazaar) and it felt light, but cool. On the left as you entered was the counter, with various glass shelves reflecting the light and a barricade of jars of pickled cucumber behind which stood the carvers, with the joint of salt beef, piles of rye bread and pots of mustard. On the right, running down the entire wall that faced the counter was a shelf, just wide enough for a plate and a glass of tea, with a row of chrome-legged bar stools.

Above the shelf ran a mirror, about eighteen inches high, one of the best placed mirrors in the world. It enabled Mark, who was short, to see everything that went on in the place without turning round, but it was sufficiently low that solitary diners, sitting at the shelf, didn't look into their own tired eyes: it reflected them from the neck down. From one of the tables, on the other hand, you could see their faces and they could see you. The mirror enlarged the place, reflected light and offered intriguing vistas.

Above the mirror, the wall was covered with black and white photographs of boxers, comedians and assorted stars, a galaxy of East End heroes and heroines, all signed with a scrawl across the corner, 'To Mark, with best wishes', sometimes with a date and a brief note of the occasion, a charity dinner or boxing match. The series went back thirty or forty years.

There were four or five small tables and I always used to sit in the corner with my back against the wall, facing down the length of the little café to the street. I could watch the proprietor, just inside the door, as he scribbled on mysterious scraps of paper or read the newspaper, constantly interrupted by passers-by who would pop their heads round the door to say hello. Others would come in and stand talking for a few minutes before going on their way. This stream of people represented the community of those who lived and worked in Soho, running the newsagents, the food shops and the restaurants or manning the stalls in Berwick Street Market, quite separate from the changing population of thugs who operated the strip shows and the clip joints, or the newcomers in films, design and advertising.

The clientele at Carrolls was mostly regular and local.

There would be an elderly Jewish couple sitting in the corner, a young black from the garage at the top of the street, a fellow from the bookmakers. Often it was empty, or nearly so, because I tended to go at quiet times of the day, at three in the afternoon.

It felt like an oasis, peaceful and unchanging, with the gaudy life of the street passing outside the windows: tourists and pimps, taxis inching up the road with their fares, the girls standing in the doorway of the strip club opposite, flashing neon signs, the drunks and the policemen. At my corner table, with a bowl of chicken soup and *kreplach*, a plate of beef and *latkas*, a glass of lemon tea, I watched the world go by.

Carrolls is gone. I went back there one day and couldn't find it. The site was boarded up and derelict, awaiting redevelopment. I asked one of the girls, shivering in the doorway opposite, what had happened. 'I dunno love,' she said. 'D'you wanna come inside?'

Potato Cakes

Latkas are simply potato cakes, made with grated potatoes, rather than mashed.

I love potato cakes and there are lots of interesting versions. It is also an excellent way of using up left-over potatoes.

The basic recipe is simple: boil and mash the potatoes (or mash left-over spuds), mix with an egg, flour, salt and black pepper and mould *lightly* with your floury fingers into round cakes, two or three inches in diameter and half an inch thick. Fry until golden brown in olive oil.

Additions. Crisply fried onion and bacon, chopped small; plenty of parsley; smoked haddock, poached and flaked; cayenne pepper or a little curry powder.

The combination of *all* these ingredients is delicious, a meal in itself. Serve with green salad.

Suggested Wine Good pink wine is lovely to look at and delicious to drink. With fishy potato cakes, I suggest Bardolino Chiaretto from Fraterna Portalupi or Château Thieuley, Bordeaux Clairet. You have to be that specific with rosé; the bad stuff is dreadful.

DOG'S DINNER

There is a family photograph taken when I was one, which shows me sitting at my mother's feet, staring imperiously at the camera, and leaning in somewhat Roman style on the head of a long-suffering dog. This wonderful beast was a mixture of boxer and South African ridgeback, the tawny colour of a lion, warm, comfortable and, we firmly believed, of enormous intelligence. Butch could, after all, manage to unlatch the scullery window (nose for the top latch, paw for the bottom) in order to escape for midnight excursions and he awoke instantly from the deepest sleep at the mention of a bone. We knew that he was no hunter (his squashed nose resulted, apparently, in a defective sense of smell) but we were confident of his courage.

It was years before I realized that this heroic hound was, like elephants, afraid of mice. One of our favourite games was to say 'Rats, rats,' and point to the corner of the room. Butch would give a convincing imitation of alert enthusiasm, sniffing vigorously at the skirting board, growling quietly and jumping around in pursuit of an imaginary rodent. When the real thing appeared, a tiny field mouse that was sheltering from the winter under the nursery floor boards, the dog leapt in terror onto the sofa. The mouse, thoroughly confused, ran after him whereupon Butch jumped onto the rocking chair, teetered wildly, and then lost his balance and crashed to the floor. As he climbed groggily to his feet we saw the tiny, squashed body of the mouse lying dead. By fatal chance the dog had sat on it.

After this shameful show of panic, it took weeks for Butch to recover his pride. If ever again we tried to get him to play the game, muttering 'Rats, rats' and pointing at the mouse hole, Butch would look at us with a mournful and accusing air, indicating in the clearest possible way that our wretched joke meant, for him, the revival of a painful memory.

The dog grew old and eventually died, so we were left with Archibald the marmalade cat and Donald Duck. The cat had the habits of a confirmed and slightly cantankerous bachelor. It dozed for most of the day on a faded red sofa in the hall, stretching from time to time in a shaft of sunlight before turning round and going back to sleep. It did not like to be disturbed. The duck, by contrast, was a lively if rather messy pet. It was a Muscovy that had been a sickly duckling and which my sister and I had raised in a cardboard box beside the stove. Eventually it recovered, though it could not fly, but it showed no signs of returning to family life on the pond. On the contrary, it continued to expect regular meals and to treat the house as its own.

One day the duck climbed up onto the red sofa and sat in the opposite corner to the cat. Archibald hissed to show his disapproval but was too dozy to bestir himself further. Donald quacked a couple of times, tucked his beak under a wing and went to sleep. This became a regular habit. After a few days in which they continued to hiss and quack, like disgruntled clubmen after lunch, the cat and duck appeared to accept each other's company.

When Archibald took his afternoon constitutional, walking down to the fig tree and back again, Donald went too. This unlikely pair became inseparable and the duck grew fat.

Then my mother got a new dog. After the leonine splendour of Butch, the choice of a snapping, yapping, restless little dachshund seemed a decided let down. It chewed slippers and books, bit ankles and fingers, and rushed around on its tiny legs in a state of constant excitement. After the first week it was generally regarded as a nuisance and we children were particularly disgusted. It was no substitute for Butch whose only violent act in his life had been to sit on a mouse.

Archibald and Donald were equally disapproving. The cat would hiss, fur on end, and the duck quacked and flapped its wings, trying to drive the dachshund away. They were particularly upset by the newcomer's company on their afternoon walks, since it jumped around in the most irritating manner and disturbed their peaceful promenade with its high pitched yelps. As it grew bigger, it even started to bite at Donald who beat it off with much squawking and pecking. What they didn't realize was that not only was the dachshund a nuisance, it was also dangerous.

One day there was a tremendous commotion under the fig tree. We rushed out but arrived too late. There were feathers everywhere, drops of blood and the dachshund dashing off with the carcass of the duck. Donald was dead but his spirit lived on. The dachshund grew fat and slothful and spent the days sitting on the red sofa with Archibald the cat. They went for their daily constitutional together, down to the fig tree and back, and the dog no longer jumped around but waddled like a duck. Its bark, formerly so sharp, became suspiciously like a quack.

A Pike in the Basement

When my mother realized that the metamorphosis was irreversible, she got a Dalmatian. This, it turned out, had an addiction to cheese soufflé.

Stuffed Duck

The best thing to do with duck (wild or tame) is to bone it and stuff it, because the flesh tends to dry out when cooked and it's fiddly to carve. The labour of boning is not great – it simply needs patience and a small sharp knife.

Lay the duck on a board, breastbone down, and cut a line through the skin from top to tail. Chop off the wings. Gently scrape the skin and flesh away from each side of the carcass until you get to the junction of legs and body. Carefully cut through the sinews etc. which hold the joints in place. Continue scraping away, keeping the knife close to the carcass and being particularly careful when you get to the breastbone (where there is only a layer of skin, which should not be pierced). Lift out the carcass and use it to make stock. Carefully scrape the flesh back from the thigh bones and disjoint from the drumsticks. You are left with a spread-out boneless duck, with two drumsticks sticking out at the sides.

If it is a reared duck (as opposed to teal or mallard) there may be a fair amount of fat which should be removed, as far as possible.

Make a stuffing with softened onions, breadcrumbs, slithers of baked orange zest, diced cooked bacon and chicken, chopped mushrooms, juice of the orange, chopped fresh thyme, salt and pepper. Spread on the boned duck. In a line down the centre, lay a few halved, uncooked fresh lambs' kidneys, carefully trimmed. Sew the whole thing up again, so that it looks like a limp duck, and roast in the oven, basting frequently with pan juices and wine. Miraculously, it should reassume the shape of a duck. It is good hot, but better cold, carved crosswise to present a circle of duck, enclosing a round of stuffing.

Serve with mashed potatoes (mixed with yoghurt) and a sprig or two of watercress.

Suggested Wine Despite the watercress (regarded by some as incompatible with fine wine) this is an occasion for good claret. The wine can be reasonably young (say ten years old) but should be splendid. I should like to drink Château d'Angludet, Chasse Spleen or Grand Puy Lacoste – wines which combine vigour and elegance.

IN PRAISE OF PIGS

My favourite sporting print depicts a man in eighteenth century attire, out shooting in the woods, accompanied by an enormous black pig, trotter raised, snout sniffing eagerly for game.

This delightful image is found in the pages of the Reverend William Daniel's *Rural Sports*, the classic three volume work on hunting, shooting and fishing, published in 1807. The text that accompanies the engraving is so intriguing that I give it here in full, the tale of a pig called Slut.

Of this most extraordinary Animal, will be here stated a short History, to the Veracity of which there are hundreds of living Witnesses: – SLUT was bred in, and was of that sort which maintain themselves in the *New Forest* without regular feeding, except when they have young, and then but for a few Weeks, and was given when about three Months old, to be a Breeding Sow, by Mr. THOMAS, to Mr. RICHARD TOOMER, both at that time Keepers in the Forest. From having no young, she was not fed, or taken very little notice of, until about eighteen months old, was seldom observed near the Lodge, but chanced to be seen one day when Mr. EDWARD TOOMER was there. The Brothers were concerned together in breaking Pointers and Setters, some of their own breeding, and others which were sent to be broke by different Gentlemen; of the latter, although they would *stand and back,* many were so indifferent, that they would neither *hunt* nor express any Satisfaction when Birds were killed and put before them. The slackness in these Dogs first suggested the Idea, that by the same Method any other animal might be made to *stand,* and do as well as one of those huntless and inactive pointers. At this instant the Sow passed by, and was remarked as being extremely handsome: R. TOOMER threw her a piece or two of Oatmeal Roll, for which she appeared grateful, and approached very near; from that time they were determined to make a *Sporting Pig* of her. The first step was to give her a *Name,* and that of SLUT (given in consequence of soiling herself in a Bog) she acknowledged in the course of the Day, and never afterwards forgot. Within a *Fortnight,* she would find and point *Partridges* or *Rabbits,* and her Training was much forwarded by the abundance of both which were near the lodge; she daily improved, and in a few Weeks would RETRIEVE Birds that had ran, as well as the best pointer; nay, her nose was superior to any Pointer they ever possessed, and no two Men in England had better. They hunted her principally on the Moors and Heaths. SLUT has stood *Partridges, Black-game, Pheasants, Snipes,* and *Rabbits* in the same day, but was never known to point a HARE. She was seldom taken by choice more than a mile or two from the Lodge, but has frequently joined them when out with their Pointers, and continued with them several Hours. She has sometimes stood a *Jack Snipe,* when all the Pointers had passed by it. In consequence of the Dogs not liking to hunt when she was with them, (for they dropped their *Sterns,* and shewed Symptoms of Jealousy,) she did not very often accompany them, except for the Novelty; or when she accidentally joined them in the Forest. Her pace was mostly a TROT, was seldom known to *Gallop,* except when called to go out Shooting, she would then come home off the Forest at full Stretch, (for she was never shut up, but to prevent her being out of the Sound of the *call or whistle,* when a party of Gentlemen had appointed to see her out the next Day, and which Call she obeyed as readily as a Dog,) and be as much elevated as a Dog upon being shewn the *Gun*. She always expressed great pleasure when Game, either dead or alive, was placed before her. She has frequently stood a single Partridge at *forty yards* distance, her Nose in a direct line to the Bird: after *standing* some considerable time, she would *drop* like a *setter*, still keeping her Nose in an exact Line, and would continue in that Position until the Game moved: if it took wing, she would come up to the place and put her Nose down two or three times; but if a Bird ran off, she would get up and go to the place, and draw slowly after it, and when the Bird stopped she would stand it as before. The two Mr. TOOMERS lived about seven miles apart, at *Rhinefield* and *Broomey* Lodges; SLUT has many times gone by herself from the one Lodge to the other, as if to court the being taken out Shooting. She was about *five years* old when her Master died, and at the Auction of his Pointers, &c. was included in the Sale, and bought in at *Ten Guineas*. Sir H. MILDMAY having express-ed a Wish to have her, she was sent to Dogmersfield Park, where she remained some years; she was last in the possession of Col. SIKES, and was then *Ten years* old, and had become fat and slothful, but would point Game as well as before. When killed, which was at Bassilden House, SLUT weighed *seven hundred pounds:* her Death, to those who possess common feelings of Humanity, appears, (if one may use the Ex-pression,) at least *Animal Murder*; it would have cost but a trifling Sum to have fed and sheltered her in the *Winter*, and the Park would have supplied her Wants during *Summer* at no Expence.

Alas poor Slut. This Shandean footnote is typical of those country vicars, heirs to Laurence Sterne and Gilbert White, who produced in the eighteenth and nineteenth centuries so many memorable volumes of natural and local history, wandering from one digression to the next: as Daniel on rural sports, so Houghton on fishes and Morris on birds and their nests, on butterflies and moths and English country houses. And it seems that those few clergymen who didn't write books kept pigs; a clerical enthusiasm that persists to the present day. Dreaming of Mermaid, his prize-winning Berkshire sow, and of Clarence, the boar whom he named in honour of Lord Emsworth, the Archbishop of Canterbury may drift back in memory to the sty where, in former days, he was often to be found 'draped like a wet sock over the rail', in the immortal words of Wodehouse.

Nowhere is this conflict between God and Gammon more endearingly expressed than in the pages of Arthur Mee's wonderfully eccentric compendium, the *Children's Encyclopaedia*. A short article on the birth of Christ ('the Greatest Event in History') is immediately preceded by a hymn to the hog which is by far the longest section in the entire ten volume work. *Pigs and Hippos* is the title of this neglected masterpiece.

The anonymous author begins with a startling vision of primaeval England, 'What a change it must have been from the humdrum of chipping flints to go to the marsh, cry "Tig, Tig, Tiggie" and see a moving mountain lurch up from the ooze and reveal himself as a hippopotamus. That was Britain indeed.'

The besotted fellow explains that 'the hippo is only a pig, a monstrous river pig, and his ancestors here were mightier in size than he. In Britain there were giants in those days.' There were also wild boar, now extinct, the ancestors of the domestic pig. The boar were protected, to be hunted by kings, but the pig was the poor man's chief possession. 'The pig was England's scavenger. We had no sanitary system; the pigs were the dustmen. They cleared the streets by eating everything that could be eaten. Therefore they were cheap to keep. In the autumn there were woods to which they could be taken for grass and beechmast and acorns.'

In Praise of Pigs

The 'lean and scraggy pigs' of those days were bred with other strains and evolved into animals of enormous size, amazingly efficient at converting food to flesh. The awestruck author describes the Large White Yorkshire Pig ('there is something almost plant-like in its tremendous growth'), the Berkshire ('famous with breeders abroad to whom we send it because its black skin will not blister in the sun as white breeds do') and 'the huge Lincolnshire Curly-coated, which rivals the Large White for weight and development and is as fascinating in its ugliness as a bulldog'. These effortlessly superior hogs now roam the world, since 'Europe has taken their pigs wherever civilization has set up house. Australia, of course, had none of any sort. America only had a little wild forest pig called the Peccary.'

There is a wealth of benign prejudice in such phrases, reminiscent of P. G. Wodehouse, and the resemblance is especially marked when the writer returns to his starting point, the hippo.

Hippo is more at home on water than on land. He does come ashore, of course, he comes out at night, pounding along like a sort of stealthy earthquake. If we may say that such a monster creeps, he does it. He creeps timidly, in his huge hippo way, to the cultivated fields of the natives, and converts a load of sugar cane or growing corn into a toothsome supper . . .

Madame hippo is a very kindly mother. The sire may be rather a turk as a parent, but she is as gentle in her vast cumbersome way as a motherly old hen with her chickens. She plays with her babe like a dog. She takes it into the water with her and teaches it its business, the whole art and mystery of hippo life.

If the water is deep and the little one is tired of trotting at her side, she lets it scramble on her mighty back.

Then comes the coda, rapturous but elegaic.

The hippos are a doomed race. Civilization is bound to destroy them in its stride. Gardens will grow where they now tramp by night; steamers will ply where they now revel and hide by day. They will disappear from Africa as they have disappeared from England.

But the future will hardly forgive the destruction of the waning few, wonderful, bizarre and fascinating, in the African twilight where so much life has been sacrificed to the determination of men to live where animals have done pioneer work.

These words are tearjerkers. I used to dream of keeping a pet hippo, wallowing in the marshes of the flooded estuary that surrounds our house, and was disappointed as a child that my parents didn't share my enthusiasm. The closest that we got was Big Ears, a huge pig which lived in a yard near the kitchen. It was post-war rationing that caused my father to turn farmer (he also tried rearing chickens, with disastrous results) and we were always aware that our pet was destined for the chopping block. When back legs buckled under the strain of his enormous weight, he was sent off to be converted into sausages. Our hearts were torn between sentiment and satisfaction.

Big Ears in his prime was a tremendous sight, a mass of contented pig shaded by two drooping flaps, and I realize now that we should have entered him in the Suffolk Show. He might even have challenged that legendary Berkshire sow, the Empress of Blandings, three times winner in the Fat Pigs class at the Shropshire Agricultural Show and pride of Lord Emsworth's heart. According to his lordship (quoting Wolff-Lehman) the diet of a champion should consist of 'barley meal, maize meal, linseed meal and separated buttermilk. I occasionally add on my own initiative a banana or a potato.'* Big Ears grew

* P. G. Wodehouse, *A Pelican at Blandings*

plump on a much less carefully balanced menu (kitchen scraps and pigmeal) and Lord Emsworth would have been horrified to read the assertion of the *Children's Encyclopaedia* that pigs 'eat anything, from carrion to corn, from snakes to sugar cane. They are all said to be able to withstand the effects of snake poison and certainly a snake is a titbit to all known species.' But I doubt whether even a pig replete with snake could be happier than those fattened by Adnams Brewery, whose daily intake consists mostly of surplus yeast and waste beer. They push with enthusiasm to the trough and afterwards, like well-fed gentlemen, take a quiet nap.

Concentrating on food, the conversion of pig to pork, most authorities on the subject ignore the animal's brain. The peasants of Perigord have proved that the pig is trainable, teaching him to find black truffles buried amongst the roots of oak trees, but scientists dismiss this evidence of intelligence, claiming that the pig is sexually attracted to the truffle. They accept the colloquial equation of 'pig-headed' with stubborn stupidity. Slut, that clever sporting pig, might have grunted expressively at such presumptions but she seemed, increasingly, a creature of distant myth. I came to believe that her story could have no sequel, that it stood alone, a unique marvel of its day. Then I heard an echo, a whisper from Wales. There was talk of pigs pursuing sheep across the meadows of the Gower Peninsular. The reality was even stranger.

There were seven brothers with seven forges, the blacksmiths of Gower. Their names were Lancelot, Cecil, Hubert, Messina, Abraham, Jasper and Bert – chosen by their father, Thomas Watters, from serial stories in the church magazine. In 1933 Hubert bought Lake Farm, at

Llandewi, and hauled his twelve-year-old son out of
school to look after the pigs.

The family has been there ever since and they have
never thrown anything away. Every surface and corner
of the old vicarage which Clive and Ian Watters share
with their mother is piled with papers and boxes and
assorted clutter. There is a small clear space between the
kitchen table and the stove and it's possible for one person
at a time to get to the telephone in the former vicar's
study, picking his way carefully past a couple of chain-
saws and some elderly cans of paint.

Much the same is true on the farm. Finding it increasingly difficult to make a livelihood from the land,
Clive Watters rearranged the accumulated agricultural
debris of three generations, put up a notice 'Gower Farm
Museum', and started charging admission. Strewn
around the modest farmyard and filling a series of stone
sheds is an astonishing collection of rusting iron, over
1800 items, all but seventy of which are from the family
hoard. Visiting the place would be about as interesting as
sorting through a scrapyard, were it not for the fact that
this is a minefield of curiosities and unexpected delights.
Tread warily.

I was chatting to Clive Watters in the yard when I
noticed that an extremely hairy snout with a ring in it was
sniffing with interest at his shopping basket and I found
myself scratching the back of a wild boar.

Wild Boar? According to the *Children's Encyclopaedia*
the boar has been extinct in the British Isles for centuries.
They say that its domestication was one of the triumphs
of primaeval man. Yet here was this enormous bristly
black animal, wandering in from the meadows with the
amiable curiosity of a large dog.

'It was a bit of a leg pull for the vet, really, but it turned out very well.' The brothers breed German Shepherds, not to mention donkeys, Shetland ponies, rabbits and ducks and ferrets and chickens and West African Pigmy Goats. 'We did think of buffalo, for the meat you see.'

The vet remarked that all their animals, including the cattle, were pets. The brothers took this as a challenge and decided to tame something really difficult.

A few weeks later they were at a sale of rare breeds, trying to choose between a bad-tempered Highland Cow and a couple of wild cats, when they noticed that all the visitors were crowding round a pen of European Wild Boar. So they bought a pair of three-month-old sisters, added a couple of Tamworth Sows (huge gingery monsters, the most closely related of all pigs to the boar) and headed back home to Llandewi.

Then they rang up the vet and asked him to come and put rings in the noses of the piglets that they'd brought back from market. 'The family is known for being a little bit of a rogue, fond of a joke,' explains Clive.

It was six months before the boars would let the brothers rest a hand on them, even at full trough, and nine before they could be stroked and handled freely. Now they will stretch out in the field for Clive to scratch their stomachs. 'They get very jealous,' says he.

That's the least of their problems. These pigs think they're sheepdogs.

It began by accident. When the brothers went out with their dogs in the winter, to bring in the sheep from the fields, the pigs went too, 'not walking at heel as a dog would do but at a tangent on either side, twelve or fifteen feet out, and very effectively they would drive the sheep along. It's a very family-minded animal, a bit like a duck.' I was reminded of my childhood pet, the Muscovy called Donald.

Now the brothers leave the dogs behind and rely on the porkers, calling 'Honky, Honky' as they summon them to work. 'They can run at speeds of up to forty five miles an hour. They're like the cheetah, it's very similar to a pig. It will sit quiet but when it makes its rush it's there. The sheep will go in short and sharp if you can find them.' They probably have nightmares.

'Although the pig is a grazing animal and the dog is a hunting animal, the trainability of both is similar. And these pigs are wonderful as guard dogs. They accept the norm but if there is anything unusual they're attentive.'

Anything unusual. Clive's idea of the norm is addictive but when I left it seemed like emerging from a curious dream. This corner of Wales is already strange enough, with its ancient stone circles, winding sunken lanes and meadows dropping over cliffs to the sea, but the Watters brothers have made of it something stranger still, a surreal world, Llandewi magnified to fill the mind. If you look too closely at almost anything it assumes odd proportions. Within the invisible boundaries of their imagination, Clive and Ian have transformed a small farm, a rusting pile of old tools and a bizarre collection of animals into the Museum. It is a place that teaches unexpected lessons of history.

Imagine a cold winter's day, with the rain driving in from the Atlantic across the bleak peninsular. A flock of sheep tears out of the mist, pursued by fearsome beasts, big, black, bristling and primaeval. The shock of the unexpected is replaced by recognition of the unbelievable. The mind whispers 'wild boar' as the ear catches a Welsh voice, calling through the rain. 'Honky, Honky'. It would seem like an echo, but for the absorbent dampness of the dripping day and the sight of a solitary figure, trudging home behind the flock. 'Honky,' he cries again and you realize that it is indeed an echo (through a hundred centuries) of the neolithic farmer's grunt, imitating his pig. Clive Watters, pastoral archaeologist, walks in the footsteps of his forebears, the first shepherds, for primitive man must surely have tamed the boar before the wolf. When the sheepdog's ancestor was still the shepherd's foe, prowling for prey, wild boar acted as guardians of the flock. Those which have at last returned to the fields above Llandewi are rediscovering their ancient role. 'Honky, Honky.' Man calls across the centuries to man's best friend, the faithful hog.

Sausages and Red Cabbage

A wonderful, vigorous dish for the winter. Buy a mixture of sausages, including the best locally made English bangers, plus one or two varieties of German or middle European smoked and spicy sausages, thin rather than thick. Cook the English sausages quickly to be crisp outside and then chop in half. Chop the other sausages into inch-long bits.

Sauté onion and diced bacon until lightly golden. Chop red peppers and soften in a pan with some olive oil. Cut smallish mushrooms in half and cook briefly with peppers.

Chop red cabbage, removing centre stalk, and mix in casserole with sausages, onions, bacon, peppers and mushrooms, salt and pepper, some red wine. Allow to cook briefly on top of stove, stirring frequently. Add best home-made chicken stock to just below level of mixture in the pot. Bring to boil. Cover with casserole lid and bake in medium oven for at least an hour.

Serve with small baked potatoes.

Suggested Wine This is the perfect dish for the Syrah grape, whether a modest Côtes du Vivarais (Domaine de Belvezet), an Australian Shiraz or a good Cornas from the northern Rhône. Heartwarming stuff.

A PIKE IN THE BASEMENT

Pike too immense to stir, so immense and old
That past nightfall I dared not cast
But silently cast and fished

With the hair frozen on my head.

Ted Hughes

The pike is a monster. Izaak Walton called him a tyrant and told fearful tales of his voracity as all anglers have done, awestruck by the size, ferocious jaws, cunning and longevity of this insatiable beast: as the shark in the sea, so the pike in river and pool.

The mightiest pike range from four to seven feet in length, up to seventy pounds in weight, and may live as long as a man, but legends are legion. The biggest and oldest of all is said to have been caught in 1497, in Swabia, with an engraved ring in its gill recording that it had been placed there by the Emperor Frederick II on 5th October 1230. Walton, with the true angler's appetite for a tall story, repeats this tale and others equally colourful. He writes of the pike that bit the lips of a mule which was drinking at a pond, and was caught thereby; of the pike that fought an otter for a carp; of the pike blinded by a frog. This dubious fable is attributed to 'Dubravius, a bishop of Bohemia'. Later authors added the story of the pike 'that seized the head of a swan, as she was feeding under water, and gorged so much of it as killed them both.'

Such episodes have none of the tranquil, almost somnolent mood which characterizes other fishy tales. They are miniature sermons, imbued with a Gothick sense of horror and retribution. The theme is taken from Walton's observation that 'pikes will bite when they are not hungry; but as some think even for very anger when a tempting bait comes near them.'

A classic nineteenth century example is found in the otherwise placid pages of the Reverend Houghton's *British Freshwater Fishes*. 'Dr. Genzik, of Lentz' is given as the source of the following history of the biter bit:

In 1829 I was bathing in the swimming school at Vienna with some fellow students when one of them – afterwards Dr. Gouge, who died a celebrated physician some years ago – suddenly screamed out and sank. We all plunged in immediately to his rescue, and succeeded in bringing him to the surface, and finally in getting him up on to the boarding of the bath, when a Pike was found sticking fast to his right heel, which would not loose its hold, but was killed and eaten by us all in company the same evening. It weighed thirty-two pounds. Gouge suffered for months from the bite.

Even cats are afraid of the pike. The illustrator of this book, Jonathan Gibbs, once caught an eleven pounder from a stream in Suffolk and carried it home in a bucket. Instead of the usual sniffs and squeaks of ecstacy, his cat took one look at Jonathan's pailful of pike and headed for the door, hair on end in horror. It returned, sensibly enough, when the fish had been transformed into quenelles.

The pike is the angler's ogre, beloved monster without

whom a thousand stories would lose dramatic bite. As his imagination drifts upon the water, the fisherman dreams. Reality is reshaped by the ripples of a mind at rest, far from the aggravating banality of facts, and the result is an exhilarating fable of what might have been, in a perfectly ordered world. The notorious unreliability of such tales is no hindrance to their appeal, just as the most tempting fly may not be that which mimics nature but a gaudy fantasy, extending the patterns of Darwinian evolution. The fisherman never lets an undue regard for the truth inhibit the colouring of a good story.

Hence my uncle. Murrough has scraped through the years with numerous ups and downs, his complicated love life and general air of financial insouciance being excused by a notable ability as a raconteur. Who else, when temporarily confined in the local loony bin, would have charmed the staff into addressing him as 'M'Lord' and have been thrown out, eventually, for exciting the amorous instincts of the elderly ladies? One of them, he claims, 'was discovered strolling about quite starkers in the grounds murmuring endearments to a lock of my hair (which she'd snitched by means of a pair of nail scissors while seated beside me on a sofa enjoying, I thought, the soothing voice of Sir Kenneth Clark talking about the Age of Restraint).'

Before the intervention of the Furies (bank managers, policemen and sundry creditors), Murrough used to spend a few weeks every year at Grantchester. He stayed at the Red Lion, walked, held court and entertained his friends. One of these was a doctor – 'The royal brain surgeon,' claimed Murrough, conjuring up strange visions of radical reconstruction in the Heir Apparent's cranium. He used to unwind with whisky after what were described as nerve-wracking operations. In a mis-

chievous spirit of scientific enquiry my uncle doctored
his bottle, replacing Teacher's Scotch with cold tea. The
surgeon's aunt rightly blamed Murrough for a state of
intoxication that, however induced, was indistinguish-
able from the real thing.

To relieve the strain of the scalpel, the doctor went
fishing and he would experiment with the latest and most
original lures. One day he returned from London with a
strangely exciting bait. This terrible thing had triplicate
hooks on either side and a large triplicate hook in the
tail of the shimmering spoon, with painted eyes and
coloured spots on its scales. It was American, gaudy
and expensive, and it wobbled through the water with
alluring instability.

All of which would have been more than sufficient to
seduce my uncle had he not already been bedazzled by its
name. For it was called the Ely Groper, a fact of
tremendous significance to a man who claimed to be the
rightful Earl of Ely, an Irish title that had, to his chagrin,
descended to distant cousins.

Armed with this glittering novelty, Murrough strolled
down the path to one of the Cam's shadiest pools, where
lurked a semi-legendary pike, terrorist of the river and
survivor of countless battles with the most cunning of
local anglers. It was Good Friday and out of season but it
was generally understood that such niceties didn't apply
to pike. Clad in a lightweight Italian grey suit (he has
never conceded to circumstances) the uncle cast the Ely
Groper into the shadowy stream.

'The whole river seemed to explode and I found myself
fighting the biggest fish I had ever hooked in my life,'
Murrough half rises from the chair as he remembers.

'He was caught by a hook in the gills when he veered
away at the last moment,' claims the doctor, in the

peevish tone of a man who has never forgotten that it was his rod and his Groper.

'Nonsense,' says my uncle. 'He swallowed the bait, I remember it well. Anyway, there I was with no gaff and no landing net wondering how I was going to handle this enormous fish when I heard a familiar voice. "Hello, Hello, Hello." It was the local bobby (he was actually called Bobby) and he lent a hand. Half an hour later we had landed a tremendous pike. It weighed twenty-eight pounds and when we cut it open we found that it had been eating cygnets and there were forty hooks inside it.'

Murrough was determined to have it stuffed but no taxidermist could be found so he settled instead for a photograph. As they waited for the reporter to arrive, the pike had its revenge. Wily, even in death, it slipped, he tripped and was hooked, with the Ely Groper firmly embedded in his scalp. So Murrough sat in the bar of the Red Lion with blood trickling from the wound, the gleaming eyes of the Groper flickering above his own and the corpse of the pike dripping on his knees. A growing circle of admirers plied him with whisky and hung upon his increasingly incoherent words.

'Rubbish,' cries the uncle. 'You're making it up.'

Not so, this is your own account, just as you told me, years ago. They sent for a doctor, you said, to extract the hook.

'I never said anything of the sort. Anyway, we had the photograph taken in the garden with the Fullers (who used to own the Red Lion) and the wine waiter, the Italian waiter and the chef. Then we buried the pike in the rose bed.'

Years later Murrough was living in Italy, at Fiesole, in a state of uneasy truce with his American wife.

'One day Janey said that a parcel had arrived from

England. Reggie Fuller's old mother had exhumed the pike and sent me the skeleton, beautifully wrapped up with lots of decorations around it, flowers and grasses. I was very touched. Janey, of course, thought the whole thing was completely mad.'

Fearful for her sanity, she chucked him out. Murrough returned to England and, after numerous wanderings, ended up in Cambridge. Every few weeks he takes a long walk, following the path through the meadows to Grantchester.

The ghost of the pike and the memories of his past adventures have woven closer ties than wives or mistresses. You could say that he is rooted in the place. I prefer to think that he is hooked.

Living pursued, dead the pursuer, the pike is a wily foe.

But there is one story that hints at an amorous heart behind what Ted Hughes calls 'the malevolent aged grin'. A romance on the theme of Death and the Maiden, it dates from between the wars and was told to me by Jack Pritchard (friend and patron of all those famous names of the thirties, artists and designers) whose Isokon flats in Hampstead once housed such diverse characters as Walter Gropius, Moholy-Nagy and Agatha Christie. Since Jack's memory is nowadays even less reliable than that of my uncle, the details have been washed away. Was the painter in the story Matthew Smith or Spencer Gore, the studio in Bond Street or Camden Town? No matter. Like all the best fish tales, this one has been transformed into myth.

An immense pike, wrapped in a sling and packed in ice, is being delivered from the fishmonger by two errand boys. It is intended as the centrepiece for a colourful still life: 'nature morte'.

A Pike in the Basement

In his basement studio the artist contemplates his model, with the amorous torpor that results from her nakedness, the warmth of the stove and a few glasses from the bottle of wine which is supposed to accompany the pike. She, too, seems dazed by the day.

The errand boys arrive at their destination. As they clamber down the steps from the pavement they find it hard to manage the heavy hammock of fish. The pike seems alive. With a twist it slides out of the sling and dives with all the lissom momentum of its forty-five pounds towards the studio door. Unlocked, unlatched, the door crashes open.

The amazed, fearful and delighted boys see a naked girl, writhing on the floor, embracing with her lovely legs the dappled ferocity of the giant pike. It is a vision of glory that wondrously embodies Mercutio's exuberant cry, 'O flesh, flesh, how thou art fishified!'.

Pike Quenelles

Ausonius, the Roman poet who lived near Bordeaux, wrote a great deal about fish, most of it unreliable. He claimed that the pike was of no culinary use. In England, by the reign of Edward I, the price of pike was fixed higher than fresh salmon, more than ten times the best turbot or cod. Much the same ambivalence continues to this day.

I am a pike enthusiast, especially when turned into quenelles, poached in fish stock and baked with a cheesy sauce. There are plenty of recipes in decent cookbooks, most of which sound extremely laborious. The Larousse is typical, giving instructions for endless pounding in a mortar and rubbing through a sieve. Eventually, when the reader feels exhausted and utterly discouraged, it says (without further explanation) 'The use of an electric blender can greatly facilitate this process.'

This is the key. You don't need one of the sophisticated new

141

machines, any old blender will do, and you don't need to make the quenelles as fine as a normal mousseline. They are in fact much better if fairly coarse textured. The character of the pike is lost if it is treated like salmon.

Suggested Wine The perfect wine for pike is white Hermitage or top quality white Châteauneuf-du-Pape (from Château de Beaucastel or Domaine du Vieux Télégraphe). Full flavoured, a hint of lime blossom, fresh but dense. Delicious.